NEW ENGLAND REMEMBERS

Boston's Abolitionists

Kerri Greenidge

Robert J. Allison, Series Editor

Commonwealth Editions
Beverly, Massachusetts

ISBN-13: 978-1-933212-19-7
ISBN-10: 1-933212-19-5

Library of Congress Cataloging-in-Publication Data
Greenidge, Kerri.
Boston's abolitionists / Kerri Greenidge.
  p. cm. — (New England remembers)
Includes bibliographical references and index.
ISBN 1-933212-19-5 (alk. paper)
1. Antislavery movements—Massachusetts—Boston—History—19th century. 2. Abolitionists—Massachusetts—Boston—History—19th century. 3. African American abolitionists—Massachusetts—Boston—History—19th century. 4. Boston (Mass.)—Politics and government—19th century. 5. Boston (Mass.)—Race relations—Political aspects—History—19th century. I. Title. II. Series.
F73.44.G74 2006
326'.8097446109034—dc22

                                        2006011328

Cover and interior design by Laura McFadden Design, Inc.
laura.mcfadden@rcn.com
Printed in the United States of America.

Commonwealth Editions
266 Cabot Street, Beverly, Massachusetts 01915
www.commonwealtheditions.com

Front cover: Robert Morris, courtesy of the Social Law Library, Boston.
Back cover: Smith Court, courtesy of Historic New England/SPNEA

New England Remembers series
Robert J. Allison, series editor
The Hurricane of 1938 by Aram Goudsouzian
The Big Dig by James A. Aloisi, Jr.
The Cocoanut Grove Fire by Stephanie Schorow
Sacco & Vanzetti by Eli J. Bortman
Lizzie Borden by Karen Elizabeth Carpenter
The Boston Strangler by Alan Rogers
The Boston Massacre by Robert J. Allison

The "New England Remembers" logo features a photo of the Thomas Pickton House, Beverly, Massachusetts, used courtesy of the Beverly Historical Society.

C O N T E N T S

FOREWORD

THEY WERE FEW IN NUMBER, but they shook the nation. Boston's abolitionists, black and white, mobilized in the 1820s when the economic and political power of slavery was growing. Cotton, raised by slave labor in the southern states, was the leading American export, and New England's emerging textile industry depended on this cheap raw cotton to spin into the fabrics that now made New England prosper. Cotton was king, said a South Carolina senator; the king was supported, said a Massachusetts senator, by the lords of the loom and the lords of the lash.

And yet this small group of Bostonians insisted that the nation live up to its Revolutionary creed. Were all men created equal? Was the nation founded in liberty, or was it founded on economic self-interest and exploitation? They used the press, the courts, and the legislature to awaken their fellow citizens, and created an "underground railroad" to bring men, women, and children out of slavery. And finally they triumphed.

Kerri Greenidge tells the story of Boston's abolitionists. Here we meet the uncompromising and relentless men and women who challenged the prevailing economic system of their day, and the political system that supported it, in order to secure the blessings of liberty to their posterity. We learn about Boston's black community, on the north slope of Beacon Hill, and we meet Maria Stewart and Lewis Hayden, David Walker and William Lloyd Garrison, and many others who would not equivocate nor rest until all men and women were free. Because we know a threat to freedom anywhere is a threat to freedom everywhere, New England remembers Boston's abolitionists.

Robert J. Allison, Series Editor
Boston, Massachusetts

To Ariel Gertrude King Dance

Special thanks to Dr. Robert Allison; Webster Bull and the staff of Commonwealth Editions; the Boston African-American National Historic Site; Jane Winton, Boston Public Library; Patricia Boulos, Boston Athenaeum; the Massachusetts Historical Society; the Social Law Library of Boston; Horace Seldon, Dana Smith, Jarumi Crooks, Bernadette Williams, and Ryan McNabb; and my family, Ariel, Kirsten, and Kaitlyn Greenidge. Thanks also to my wonderful husband, Christian Douglass, for all his support.

INTRODUCTION

BLACK ROOTS

THEY FIRST ARRIVED IN MASSACHUSETTS in 1638 aboard the slave ship *Desire*, and for more than a century their unpaid labor provided the fuel that kept the Bay Colony running. As dockworkers, stevedores, artisans, and servants, they had jobs as diverse as the places from which they came. By the start of the American Revolution, more than five thousand blacks called Massachusetts home, the vast majority of them living in Boston. There, in the city on a hill, they struggled to make a life for themselves in a place where the economy thrived from their subjugation.

During the eighteenth century, the New England slave trade was centered in Massachusetts, and Boston was the chief port through which the lucrative trade in human flesh was conducted. Relatively few Africans ended up in the Bay Colony after their long journey on the Middle Passage, but this did not stop merchants and businessmen from making huge profits on the trade in black lives. In 1641 Massachusetts was the first colony to legalize slavery.

Although black Bostonians were viewed as property under the law and were actively prevented from gathering on the Boston Common, from traveling where and when they wanted to, and from holding certain jobs, they—like blacks throughout the colonies—did not submit quietly to white domination. Indeed, Boston was full of signs that black men and women were a viable part of the city. It was Cotton Mather's slave, Onesimus, who introduced his master to the African practice of inoculation during the 1721 small pox epidemic. John Campbell, publisher of the *Boston News Letter*, the first permanent newspaper in the English colonies, was assisted in his printing press by his black slave. And Crispus Attucks, a man of mixed African and Native American ancestry, was the first to die in 1770 in the bloody Boston Massacre.

With the birth of American independence, black Boston grew, and so did its aspirations. In 1781 a black woman named Elizabeth "Mum

Bett" Freeman sued her master for her freedom based on the recently adopted Massachusetts Constitution. Although her case was tried outside Boston, its effects would resound forever in the hearts, minds, and lives of thousands of black people across the Bay State. By 1783 slavery was outlawed as an institution in Massachusetts, and by 1790 all the 5,369 blacks who lived in the state were free.

For black Bostonians, their rights as American citizens, and as human beings, were never in question. By 1800 they had their own Masonic order, their own church, their own school, and their own poet, in the person of Phillis Wheatley. Wheatley's 1773 book of poetry was the first book published by a black person in North America, and she became a minor celebrity in both old and New England. Some white Bostonians, however, did not accept the humanity of black people and did not believe that their rights were guaranteed by either the U.S. Constitution or the Massachusetts state legislature. Mobs of white youths continued to chase black men, women, and children from the Boston Common, regardless of the valiant efforts of black community leaders, such as Revolutionary War veteran George Middleton. Middleton reportedly carried a musket to protect his community from these assaults. Despite Horace Mann's proclamation that public education was "the greatest discovery ever made by man," black children did not attend the city's public schools, and black teachers were not trained in the Teacher's Training College. White employers refused to hire even the most highly trained black craftsmen, forcing most blacks to work in the lowest-paying, least desirable jobs in the city. Although a rare few became artisans, business owners, and professionals—Thomas Paul was a minister, Paul Cuffe a merchant, Cato Gardner a philanthropist—most black Bostonians languished in poverty.

Of course, the most glaring challenge to black freedom was the fact that slavery was legal in the rest of the country, and it was rapidly expanding as the nineteenth century began, partly owing to the invention of the cotton gin and the growth of cotton as the leading American export. The growth of the slave population as a result of the economy's increasing dependence on slave labor led to slave codes and black laws that sought the permanent subjugation of black people, slave and free, across the country.

Many white New Englanders had been questioning the morality of slavery ever since Boston judge Samuel Sewell wrote the first antislavery tract in the colonies, in 1701. Now, with the fervor of the Revolution still palpable, and the rise of Enlightenment principles, the young nation was finally ready to confront its notions of freedom and equality. The movement that began in Boston would place the city at the forefront of American social activism. And as Boston braced itself, black Bostonians, part of the city from its beginning yet rarely given a fair shake, would lead white Bostonians in their fight for American liberty.

CHAPTER ONE

Enlightening One's Brethren

WINDING UP BELKNAP STREET through the North Slope of Beacon Hill in the autumn of 1829, a current of optimism electrified the air. Black men and women heading home from the docks across Cambridge Street or the kitchens and nurseries of stately mansions on Mount Vernon and Charles streets crowded the unpaved roads and muddy cobblestone sidewalks. From the courtyard on the right, haloed in wooden structures, brick alleyways, and the neighborhood privy, students at the African School in the basement of the African Meeting House picked up their things and headed for home. Things were about to change in the city, and many in the community were hot with anticipation.

In the years since Thomas Paul's first sermon from the African Meeting House pulpit in 1806, the community had changed so much that a visitor passing through it might have thought the black community was bigger than it was. Approximately 1,875 blacks called Boston home, just over 3 percent of the total population. But more than two-thirds of them lived on the North Slope of Beacon Hill and across Cambridge Street on the docks and in the boardinghouses of the North End. They had had their own school since 1798, thanks to the work of Thomas Paul, Prince Hall, and Prince Hall's son, Primus Hall. They also had five of their own churches: two Baptist, two African Methodist Episcopal, and one African Methodist Episcopal Zion.

Smith Court on Beacon Hill, ca. 1900. On the left are the African Meeting House and the Abiel Smith School, two of the most important institutions of nineteenth-century black Boston. To the right, behind the tree, is the home of William Nell, abolitionist and crusader for school integration. In the heart of the black community, Smith Court was typical of the kinds of narrow streets, courtyards, and cul-de-sacs that dotted the North Slope during the height of the abolitionist movement. (Courtesy of Historic New England/SPNEA)

Its detractors called it "Nigger Hill" to distinguish it from the South Slope of Beacon Hill where wealthy whites resided in proper Federalist estates and genteel Victorian houses. Whereas the South Slope had estates and gardens, with windows overlooking the gold-domed State House and the lawns of Boston Common, the neighboring North Slope had dance halls and brothels, ropewalks, and dark alleyways. The North Slope held such a grim place in the popular imagination of white Boston that white parents were known to threaten naughty children that they would be sold to the black man who lived at the base of the hill.

But the community was not simply a place of lawlessness and vice. On an autumn day in 1829 a current of anticipation spread through the clothing stores and barbershops of the North Slope. One of the residents had just published a pamphlet, less than two hundred pages long, that made sailors and seamstresses tremble with excitement and fear. The author was David Walker, a black tailor originally from North

Carolina, whose house at No. 8 Belknap Street was a meeting place for black artisans and community leaders. Like many of his free countrymen in the slaveholding states, Walker had left the South as North Carolina and other states passed black laws restricting the liberty of free black men and women. He arrived in Boston in 1825 and went to work as a tailor, living with other black artisans in a boardinghouse on Southac Street, a block away from the house where Primus Hall started his school in 1798. An outspoken critic of slavery and racial oppression, Walker quickly established himself as a reform leader in Boston. He joined the May Street Methodist Episcopal Church, led by black minister Samuel Snowden. In 1826, he founded the first black-run political organization of its kind, the Massachusetts General Colored Association, which agitated for black rights in Boston and for emancipation of slaves in the South.

And now Walker had written a pamphlet, titled *An Appeal to the Colored Citizens of the World*, an impassioned espousal of black liberation. In it, Walker proclaimed that slavery in America was the most dehumanizing form of oppression in world history—for unlike slavery in ancient times, American slavery promoted the idea that blacks as a race were subhuman. As a result of slavery, Walker stated, "We coloured people of these United States are the most wretched, degraded, and abject set of beings that ever lived since the world began." Such degradation was not only inhumane, but hypocritical—after fighting for emancipation from Britain and founding a nation based on equality, white Americans continued to enslave and degrade black people across the Republic. And Walker was not afraid to take to task the esteemed founding fathers of the American government. The biggest target of his rage was President Thomas Jefferson. The very man who in the Declaration of Independence had averred that "all men are created equal" had written an essay titled *Notes on Virginia* that extolled the virtues of American democracy and independence while denying the humanity of black people.

To his readers, both black and white, Walker gave advice and warning. Blacks should not be submissive to white injustice but should resist slavery and oppression by any means. They should create independent black organizations, such as the African Freemasons and the Massachusetts General Colored Association in Boston, so that they could lift themselves out of the degradation caused by racial oppression. "We can help ourselves," he railed, "for if we lay aside abject servility and be determined to act like men . . . the murderers among the Whites would be afraid to show their cruel heads." Walker warned whites that their oppression of blacks would not go unpunished in the eyes of God, and that their destruction would come soon if they failed to live up to their professions of American liberty. Incensed with the passion of one who had witnessed southern slavery and northern discrimination, Walker shouted, "Americans! Americans!! I call God—I call Angels—I call men, to witness that your DESTRUCTION is at hand, and will be speedily consummated unless you repent."

As the *Appeal* reached the slave states through the well-organized community of free blacks from Massachusetts to North Carolina, white Southerners began to tremble. The bloody 1822 slave revolt of Denmark Vesey and his followers in Charleston, South Carolina, was still fresh in their minds, and in places where black slaves outnumbered whites, the prospect of insurrection was horrifying. One southern governor wrote to Boston mayor Josiah Quincy, demanding that he stop the presses from publishing the *Appeal*. North Carolina offered a reward for anyone who caught Walker, dead or alive. In the North, white antislavery activists dismissed the *Appeal* as violent propaganda and denounced Walker's call for black resistance. One Boston reporter questioned whether Walker, a free black man from North Carolina, had actually written the pamphlet—after all, no black man could possibly write so eloquently and so passionately about God and revenge, injustice and oppression.

Yet for black Bostonians, Walker's *Appeal* resounded like the welcome voice of redemption. As a race, they were segregated, mistreated, and sneered at—so the voice of a black man telling them to "go forth and enlighten your brethren" was the signal they needed to resume their fight for racial equality with more vigor than ever before. They read it aloud so that those who could not read could hear it, and they talked about it from the pulpits of their churches. Even after David Walker's sudden death in 1830, his *Appeal* continued to reverberate through Boston as militant organizations sprang up across the North Slope. Said the *Boston Evening Transcript* after the *Appeal* was reprinted in 1830, "We have noted a marked difference in the deportment of our colored population. It is evident they have read this pamphlet, nay, we know that the larger portion of them have read it, or heard it read, and that they glory in its principles, as if it were a star in the east, guiding them to freedom and emancipation."

One of the major social developments that had inspired Walker's scorn, and the scorn of those who admired him, was the American Colonization Society. The ACS was founded in 1816 in Washington, D.C., by Robert Finley, a white Presbyterian minister from New Jersey. To address what many white Northerners viewed as the problem of poor, uneducated free blacks, the ACS wanted to transport free blacks from the United States to western Africa. At first some blacks were attracted to the idea—the cruelty of whites, the institutionalization of racism, and the spread of black laws left many free black people looking for something that would improve their lives. In Boston, Thomas Paul and African School teacher Prince Saunders traveled to Haiti on behalf of the ACS. They were receptive to the idea of black relocation because local black mariner Paul Cuffe, one of the most successful merchants of his day, had been working with blacks from other eastern cities to create a colony on the West African coast. In Liberia, Cuffe and his black supporters hoped that blacks could gain economic independence from white Americans.

With the ACS's promotion of colonization, Paul Cuffe's dream seemed like it was about to come true. But as the years passed, the entire idea of colonization began to crumble. White colonizationists excluded blacks from the planning process. Further, unlike Cuffe, whites weren't interested in emancipation and universal freedom for American blacks; they wanted blacks out of the country, and they wanted to keep them under the economic control of white Americans. In their campaign for donations and support, many white colonizationists relied on derogatory images and racist stereotypes. Many of the ACS's white philanthropists were southern slaveholders, including Kentucky senator Henry Clay, who sought federal support for colonization. The colonies themselves were hardly successful: In Liberia, black emigrants were still controlled by white interests, and in Haiti, where Thomas Paul helped transport several black Bostonians in 1824, settlers were not prepared for the diseases or harsh living conditions of the Caribbean.

Thus, by the time David Walker started the Massachusetts General

Colored Association in 1826, black Bostonians, like their brethren throughout the North, distrusted colonization schemes and white colonizationists who called themselves friends of the slaves. Most blacks saw the negative impact black emigration would have on emancipation: with free blacks sent away, whiteness would become the sign of freedom, and all black Americans would be condemned to slavery. Besides, black Americans had more than two hundred years of proud history in America. They had fought gallantly in the Revolution and in the recent War of 1812. Didn't that entitle them to the same freedoms as white Americans?

On February 15, 1831, a group of black Bostonians met at the African School in the basement of the African Meeting House to write a formal protest against colonization. Many of them had read the *Appeal* and some had known David Walker, including Rev. Samuel Snowden, pastor of the Methodist Church on May Street. The group was particularly upset that their white neighbors on the south side of Beacon Hill had recently formed a Massachusetts auxiliary to the ACS. They published a protest in the local press, calling the ACS a "clamorous, abusive, and peace-disturbing measure." They denounced clergymen, black and white, who urged their parishioners to support colonization. They also vowed to carry David Walker's vision of black redemption forward through organized opposition to racial injustice and slavery.

Before the meeting adjourned for the evening, John T. Hilton, a barber and a member of the African Freemasons who lived near Walker's former residence on Belknap Street, stood to offer a note of thanks. Although most white Bostonians either supported colonization or ignored the problem of segregation and slavery, some were sympathetic to the cause. One of these was a bespectacled newspaper editor from Newburyport, Massachusetts, named William Lloyd Garrison. Garrison had begun his career by working with antislavery editor Benjamin Lundy in Baltimore. In 1829, the same year that Walker published his *Appeal*, Garrison gave an antislavery speech sponsored by the ACS at Boston's Park Street Church.

With his arrival in Boston in 1830, however, the young Garrison's views on slavery and freedom began to change. Unlike other antislavery activists, he not only wanted to end slavery; he also wanted black Americans to have the same rights as white Americans. He supported

The African Meeting House, ca. 1900. Built in 1806, it is the oldest extant black church building in America and was the first church built by African Americans in Boston. It quickly became one of the most important institutions in antebellum black Boston. The New England Anti-Slavery Society was founded here in 1832, and many of the century's most prominent abolitionists spoke from the pulpit, including William Lloyd Garrison, Wendell Phillips, Thomas Paul, Frederick Douglass, Charles Lenox Remond, and William Nell. (Courtesy of the Boston Athenaeum)

the black community, while most whites scorned it. White antislavery crusader Julia Ward Howe, for example, called black Bostonians "coarse," "ugly," and lazy even as she wrote the words to the signal ballad of the Union cause, the "Battle Hymn of the Republic."

But Garrison was different. On January 1, 1831, he published the first edition of *The Liberator*, a weekly newspaper dedicated to the abolition of slavery—and more radically—to the rights of free blacks such as those in Boston. *The Liberator* published not only abolitionist propaganda but also advertisements, announcements, and speeches of free blacks, particularly in Boston. In this way, the newspaper provided a vehicle for black activists that hadn't been available since the 1829 demise of *Freedom's Journal*, the first black newspaper in the country, established in New York in 1827 by African School teacher John Russworm. *Freedom's Journal* provided inspiration for free blacks across the North—David Walker and John Hilton helped sell it in Boston—and it paved the way for many other black newspapers and periodicals, including Frederick Douglass's *North Star* and New York City's *Colored American*.

But *The Liberator* was unique. It lasted until after the Civil War, and during that time it reached the consciences of white and black people from Maine to South Carolina. More important, Garrison's earnest commitment to abolition and equality was a radical departure from the "gradualism" espoused by most antislavery activists and colonizationists. "I will be as harsh as truth and as uncompromising as justice," Garrison shouted from the front page of his newspaper's first issue. "I am in earnest—I will not equivocate—I will not excuse—I will not retreat a single inch—And I WILL BE HEARD."

That February night in 1831, when John Hilton stood up at the end of the anticolonization meeting at the African Meeting House, he thanked Garrison for his support. *The Liberator* was less than two months old, but already it was causing a sensation. It was one of the only white antislavery newspapers to publish the proceedings of the meeting and to encourage blacks to work as printers and copiers in Garrison's publishing office on Cornhill Street. Seven months later, after Nat Turner's bloody slave rebellion in Virginia, the state of Georgia offered a five thousand–dollar reward for Garrison and all other publishers or agents of *The Liberator*. Garrison himself was not ashamed that black readers read his paper, and for the rest of his life he proudly acknowledged the contribution of black Bostonians to its survival. More than 75 percent of his subscribers were black, and Garrison was fond of noting that they paid their subscriptions more promptly than most white readers.

Through the relationship between William Lloyd Garrison and black Bostonians, the abolition movement began to take off in Boston. This new movement had an urgency that earlier antislavery efforts lacked, partly because of Garrison's and the black community's specific ideas of how slavery could be abolished and racial equality achieved. Known as Garrisonian abolitionists, they did not believe in colonization or gradualism like other antislavery advocates. Instead, Garrisonians, many of whom had been inaugurated into the fight through Walker's *Appeal*, believed in the immediate emancipation of all black people and racial equality across American society.

Although they were militant in their beliefs, Garrison and his followers were also pacifists. They believed that slavery, like other forms of wickedness, could be exorcised only through moral suasion and other peaceful initiatives—not violence. They also opposed any government that forced citizens to participate in violence, either through war or through slavery. Garrison distrusted organized politics and the U.S. government as a whole, and he did not believe in voting—to him, such an act was akin to casting one's lot in an inherently evil system. He viewed the Constitution as a proslavery document and famously burned a copy of it during one of his lectures.

Despite his pacifism, Garrison conceded that certain forms of armed resistance against slave catchers and violent proslavery mobs were the only way for blacks and their white allies to stand up for themselves. He admired abolitionist editor Elijah Lovejoy of Illinois, who armed himself against the angry mobs who frequently destroyed his printing shop. (Lovejoy was eventually killed by such a mob in 1837.)

Some of Garrison's pacifist principles contradicted the ideas of black Bostonians. For instance, many black men and women did not see pacifism as a route to freedom. They had to wage a constant fight against whites who tried to demean them or keep them in chains. Peaceful, principled action was not enough to counter the threat of enslavement or the indignity of inequality in a world where many whites, such as Boston minister Orestes Brownson, insisted that slavery elevated blacks from their natural state of inferiority. No less a person than Harvard naturalist Louis Agassiz, perhaps Boston's most noted scientist, theorized that the African brain was much smaller than the European, and therefore that blacks had a limited capacity to learn and absorb the complexities of civilization, particularly the concept of freedom. Many slaveowners and proslavery advocates used these theories to justify their violence against blacks. How, then, could black people, slave or free, sit back and advocate peace, when all the whites around them seemed to consider them subhuman? Hadn't David Walker himself advocated black self-defense against white oppression?

Garrison, of course, did not mean for black men to be inactive against persecution. After all, he had been one of the only white men to empathize with Walker's *Appeal* even as his colleagues dismissed it as a violent call for black revenge. He had read the *Appeal*, and like black readers, he was moved by it. He might not agree with Walker's espousal of violent self-defense but, he stated, "It is not for the American people . . . to denounce it as bloody or monstrous. . . . If any people were ever justified in throwing off the yoke of their tyrants," he concluded, "the slaves are that people."

If Garrison's pacifism was hard for some blacks to swallow, then his opposition to and distrust of the government was even harder to reconcile. Many blacks were proud of their role in helping to fight for a

William Lloyd Garrison (left) and Wendell Phillips, faithful stalwarts of the abolitionist movement. Garrison, editor of **The Liberator,** *had an uncompromising devotion to the complete emancipation of enslaved African Americans. Wendell Phillips, the son of Boston's mayor, was a powerful orator whose speeches appealed to both intellectuals and the common man. Phillips continued to work for racial equality even after slavery ended in 1865. (Courtesy of the Boston Public Library)*

nation founded on liberty and equality. When Garrison burned the Constitution, they understood his sentiment and applauded his daring, but they disagreed with the idea that the American system was inherently flawed. It was precisely because the American system advocated equality and liberty that they were dissatisfied with slavery and racial oppression—the principles of the Declaration of Independence and the Revolution provided the main thrust to their argument against racial proscription. Unlike Garrison, many blacks wanted to work for their rights within the American system, not outside it.

Garrison heeded his followers' opinions while holding to his principles. He continued to argue that the Constitution was a slaveholders' document and argue that voting was an act of complicity in the system that protected slavery, but he also encouraged his journalists, many of them black, to cover local political campaigns. He even listed the location of polling stations across the city and made suggestions on which candidates were more sympathetic to black interests.

Garrison's ability to support the black community on issues like militant resistance and political agitation while adhering to his own views garnered him a high level of respect among black Bostonians. When an angry proslavery mob attacked and nearly killed Garrison during a speech in 1835, black members of the crowd were among the first to try to protect him. When Susan Paul, Thomas Paul's daughter and a teacher at the African School, founded a chorus of black children to sing and raise money for the antislavery cause, she named them the Juvenile Garrison Choir. They often sang for wealthy white philanthropists who donated money to the cause.

Despite their disagreement with some of his methods, black Bostonians overwhelmingly supported both *The Liberator* and the New England Anti-Slavery Society, which Garrison and other white abolitionists established in 1832. The society, which met in the African Meeting House, disseminated abolitionist literature, sponsored speaking tours, and organized abolitionists throughout New England. Although all of its initial members were white, blacks played an important role in the NEASS: it was their church that hosted the historic inaugural meeting, and more than one-fourth of those who signed the society's constitution were black. The Massachusetts General Colored Association, founded six years before the NEASS, was granted affiliate status. Over the years, the New England Anti-Slavery Society, and its cousins, the American and Massachusetts Anti-Slavery Societies, would do more to awaken the conscience of America than any other organizations of their time.

σ♂   σ♂   σ♂

IF BLACK BOSTONIANS STILL FELT a conflict between their own needs and the ideology of their most outspoken white ally, they needed only look to a member of their own community to help bridge the gap.

Maria Walker Stewart was a writer, a lecturer, and an activist from Hartford, Connecticut. As a child, she was orphaned and sent to work for a white clergyman and his family, who taught her how to read the Bible. In 1826 she married Boston businessman James Stewart, whose shipping company on Broad Street provided her with a comfortable life as a member of the North Slope's small black middle class. The Stewarts were well known and respected in the community. Thomas Paul officiated over their marriage at the African Meeting House; James Stewart was a friend and supporter of David Walker—and a founding member of the Massachusetts General Colored Association. The Stewarts even lived for a time in Walker's home on Belknap Street. When the *Appeal* was published in 1829, Maria Stewart was one of the thousands of black people electrified by Walker's vision; she read it and reread it and bought copies for friends. Inspired by its words, and convinced that she was transformed by a call from God, she devoted herself to the cause of racial equality.

After her husband died suddenly in December 1829, Maria Stewart saw firsthand the evils of Boston racism. In his will, James Stewart left money and property to his wife, but the court system seized it, falsely claiming that Stewart owed money to the city. David Walker spoke about this ill treatment of Stewart during his speeches, using it as an example of how poorly blacks were treated even in a state as liberal as Massachusetts. When Walker died in 1830, Maria Stewart was alone and near poverty, but she began to write essays and speeches in the same vein as Walker. "How long shall the fair daughters of Africa be compelled to bury their minds and hearts beneath a pile of iron pots and kettles?" she asked. "Possess the spirit of men, bold and enterprising, fearless and undaunted. . . . If no one will promote or respect us, let us promote and respect ourselves."

In the fall of 1831, Stewart arrived at Garrison's office at No. 11 Merchants' Hall with a manuscript. Almost half a century later, Garrison recalled his first impression of her intelligence and "excellence of character." He agreed to publish her writings in *The Liberator* and to help compile them into a book, *Religion and the Pure Principles of Morality*, published in 1832. In it, and through a series of speeches she gave throughout Boston to promote the book, Stewart helped readers bridge the gap between the radicalism of David Walker and the pacifism of

William Lloyd Garrison. She called on black people to "sue for your rights and privileges!" She exhorted the "brave spirit of David Walker" and the courage of black men who fought against white oppressors. Yet she also stated that black people needed to uplift themselves from degradation and poverty. Like Garrison, whose poverty-stricken, Baptist background made him pious and principled, Stewart believed that the true route to black manhood was through strength of character and the development of morality. "Let us not imitate these Caucasian vices!" she exclaimed, and she admonished blacks for spending money at dance halls and on alcohol. Couldn't that money be saved to start a black training school or business?

In Maria Stewart, black Bostonians found a leader capable of articulating the various means of achieving racial equality . She also was a woman who shattered prevailing notions of gender. She became the first American-born woman of any race to speak before a mixed audience of men and women on a political subject. She founded the Afric-American Female Intelligence Agency to inspire black women to start their own abolition society. "What if I am a woman?" she boldly asked. In her second book of speeches, she traced the contribution of women activists throughout history, beginning with women from ancient and biblical times, such as Deborah, Mary Magdalene, the sibyls, and the oracles. She was not afraid to challenge members of the premier black male organization in Boston, the Prince Hall Masons, exhorting them to spend less time in pomp and ritual and more time fighting the evils of racial oppression. For such boldness, Stewart was driven from Boston amid slander and controversy—many black men believed that she had overstepped the long-established boundaries of female submission by daring to criticize black male leaders. She eventually went to Baltimore, and then New York, where she taught school. After the Civil War, Garrison helped her republish her speeches.

Boston might not have been ready to hear the uncompromising voice of a black woman such as Maria Stewart, but by articulating the link between Walker's radicalism and Garrisonian activism, she helped establish militant abolition as the major force in black Boston during the 1830s. With black Bostonians acting as lieutenants in Garrison's crusade against slavery, and with Garrison acting as the mouthpiece for black agitation for racial equality, Boston was about to change forever.

CHAPTER TWO

Toward Greater Equality

A DECADE AFTER THE FOUNDING of the New England Anti-Slavery Society, the African Meeting House was again buzzing with activity. During the last days of October and the first days of November 1842, candles glowed in the windows late into the night as hordes of people, black and white, crowded the second floor to hear Frederick Douglass, Charles Lenox Remond, Wendell Phillips, and other speakers voice their outrage at a recent horrible injustice. On October 20, a fugitive slave from Virginia named George Latimer had been arrested and jailed in Boston. After his master, John Gray, applied to the Massachusetts Supreme Judicial Court for a certificate to return Latimer to slavery in Virginia, a hearing was set to determine whether Latimer would indeed be sent back to slavery. George Latimer languished, frightened and alone, in the local jail while Gray went to Norfolk to get papers to prove that Latimer was his slave.

Abolitionists were outraged. How could a man be held in jail when he had not been charged with a crime? George Latimer's future hung in the balance, and he had not even been assigned an attorney. Almost immediately, members of the Massachusetts Anti-Slavery Society sent one of their attorneys, Ellis Gray Loring, to meet with him.

A descendant of one of the oldest and most respected white families in Boston, Loring was one of the original members of Garrison's New England Anti-Slavery Society. Now, as counsel for the Massachusetts

Anti-Slavery Society, his job was to use the law to defend the abolitionist cause. When he met George Latimer, he began building a case to take to the Massachusetts Supreme Judicial Court. First he filed two appeals on Latimer's behalf—a writ of personal replevin and a writ of habeas corpus. The basis of Loring's argument was that Latimer had never gone before a jury and that therefore he should be freed.

When both of these efforts failed, abolitionists all across the city organized mass protests against Latimer's capture. Night after night, crowds of indignant blacks and whites met at the African Meeting House to raise money to purchase Latimer's freedom. To keep the community rallied behind Latimer's defense, they published a special newspaper, the *Latimer and North Star Journal*, which kept the public abreast of what was going on in the courthouse. When John Gray returned from Virginia, he changed his mind, demanding four hundred dollars in exchange for Latimer's freedom. The black community accepted the offer, and George Latimer walked out of the Boston jail a free man.

But the protest did not stop there. The case had brought home the horrible fact that southern blacks, most of whom fled north with nothing but the clothes on their backs, were vulnerable to kidnappers. In addition, Southerners with ties to the Bay State were not shy about challenging the state's emancipation laws by bringing their slaves with them to the city while visiting relatives or conducting business. Abolitionists

Ellis Gray Loring, an attorney who fought against slavery and racial injustice. Descended from the wealthy white aristocracy, Loring was a mentor to black attorney Robert Morris. As attorney for the New England Anti-Slavery Society, Loring argued on behalf of the slave child Med and fugitive slave George Latimer, and later assisted the Boston Vigilance Committee. (Courtesy of the Massachusetts Historical Society)

had confronted this blatant disregard of Massachusetts law by prosecuting white Southerners who came to the Bay State with their slaves. In 1836 there was a case involving a six-year-old slave girl from Louisiana, who was brought to Boston when her mistress visited relatives on Beacon Hill. The women of the Boston Female Anti-Slavery Society hired Ellis Gray Loring to challenge the right of the slaveowner to take the girl, named Med, back to Louisiana. Loring won the case, and Med was eventually set free.

Although the court had ruled in favor of Med, that didn't stop slave catchers from prowling the streets of Boston in search of blacks to return to slavery. The U.S. Constitution, after all, protected the rights of property, and men like John Gray had every right to come to Boston and lay claim to men like George Latimer. The Latimer case proved that the laws protecting the freedom of black Bostonians were weak. The fight for full equality, therefore, could not end simply because George Latimer was free.

Immediately following the George Latimer case, black Bostonians took the lead in distributing a petition urging the state legislature to pass stricter laws protecting the rights of free people in Massachusetts. The petition contained 64,526 signatures and weighed an astonishing 150 pounds when it arrived at the State House. In response, the legislature passed the 1843 Personal Liberty Law, which banned the use of Massachusetts officials or facilities in capturing fugitive slaves.

The outcome of the George Latimer case and the passage of the Personal Liberty Law strengthened the abolitionist cause in Boston. The fact that so many people showed up to protest against Latimer's imprisonment, and that so many of them signed a petition to strengthen the rights of fugitives in Massachusetts, proved that abolitionist propaganda had influenced public opinion, at least in Boston. Garrison was right: Moral suasion was working, and it had saved a man's life. Minds were changing, albeit slowly.

The outcome of the Latimer case also proved what many of Garrison's fellow abolitionists had been trying to show: that legal action, coupled with moral suasion, was a potent antidote to inequality. Like black Bostonians who supported Garrison but questioned his methods, new converts to the abolitionist cause saw political and legal action as the only way to secure liberty for blacks. It was Loring's appeal to the law, after all, that had prevented Latimer from being extradited immediately to Virginia.

Three years before the Latimer case, in 1840, these political abolitionists had split from Garrison and founded the Liberty Party in New York, the first party of its kind to run on an antislavery platform. Many Liberty Party members had originally joined the national Whig Party, which advocated business and the rights of the state over federal intrusion. Yet many northern members of the Whig Party grew frustrated because of the party's domination by southern slave interests. As "Conscience Whigs," northern members of the party with antislavery leanings believed that slavery was immoral and that it would eventually harm political and economic interests. As members of the national Whig Party, Conscience Whigs faced an uphill battle in winning over fellow party members to their point of view. The Liberty Party gave them a voice, and many Conscience Whigs left the party to concentrate on building the Liberty Party's constituency. In both 1840 and 1844, the Liberty Party had enough members to nominate a candidate, James G. Birney, for president.

New political interests were not the only things changing the abolitionist movement in the 1840s. The issue of gender also entered the movement, as abolitionists struggled with how to handle the issue of women activists. Since Maria Stewart had challenged notions of gender and race in 1832, women of both races had been staunch supporters of the abolitionist cause. Lucretia Mott and Maria Weston Chapman founded the Boston Female Anti-Slavery Society, which took the lead in prosecuting the Med case, and by the beginning of the 1840s, women's auxiliaries to the Massachusetts and American Anti-Slavery Societies were popping up all over New England. Garrison believed that women should play an equal role with men in running the American Anti-Slavery Society, and when he, Wendell Phillips, and Frederick Douglass traveled to Europe to attend the World Anti-Slavery Conference, Lydia Maria Child and other Boston women accompanied them. Far from being the mere auxiliaries of male abolitionists, these women were smart, dedicated, and effective. For instance, Lydia Child, a well-known author whose husband, David L. Child, had attended the inaugural meeting of the NEASS, had written her own antislavery tract in 1833, *An Appeal in Favor of that Class of Americans Called Africans*.

Many men, however, believed that women should play a subordinate role in the movement, just as they played in life. And they were horrified when Garrison started to talk of emancipation for women in addition to emancipation of the slaves. Not only did this view of women go against what they saw as the natural order of things, but they also believed that Garrison was diverting attention from the issue of black freedom by concentrating on women's rights. Apparently many of the men who had split with Garrison to form the Liberty Party did not agree with Lydia Child's conclusion that issues of gender equality "did not bring [other questions] into anti-slavery, rather they came in, simply because everything in God's universe is linked with every other."

Despite their internal divisions, abolitionists never lost sight of their ultimate goal. This was especially important because on a national level their radical ideology was still a minority opinion. Slavery was spreading in the South and was now the main source of economic growth in the region. Cotton was king, and it fueled the industry of northern states, including Massachusetts. In the North, where free labor, not slavery, was the basis of economic prosperity, slavery was considered a necessary evil. It was slave labor that produced the cotton for the factories in mill towns such as Lowell and Lawrence; politically, it was cooperation between northern industrialists and their southern slaveholding counterparts that strengthened the national Whig Party.

Slavery was entrenched in all aspects of American life, and hostility toward abolitionists reached its peak in the late 1830s and the early 1840s. President Andrew Jackson called abolitionist newspapers "unconstitutional and wicked." After a proslavery mob in Alton, Illinois, killed abolitionist editor Elijah Lovejoy in 1837, Massachusetts Attorney General James T. Austin defended Lovejoy's murderers from the pulpit of Faneuil Hall. Austin believed, like most Americans, that slaveholders and those who sympathized with them were merely standing up for their property rights. In their debates about the rights of property and American economics, most white Americans ignored how slavery affected the lives of black people like George Latimer, who simply wanted their rights to freedom and equality. Clearly, in such an environment, abolitionists could not afford to be too divided—they needed one another to keep their cause alive.

Thus the split between Garrison and political abolitionists did not distract from the cause; in fact, the abolition movement's diverse methods of combating slavery attracted more people to its ranks. Many of the best reformers in Massachusetts believed wholeheartedly that slavery was morally wrong, but they also believed in the American system. They were willing to take Garrisonian principles beyond the antislavery societies and work within the American legal system to challenge the racial status quo.

One Bostonian who was particularly committed to applying abolitionist principles to the American system was Charles Sumner, a highly principled, moralistic white attorney. Sumner was born on the "wrong side of the tracks" on the North Slope of Beacon Hill. When Sumner was a boy, his father, a liberal-minded sheriff, treated his mostly black neighbors with a level of respect that was unusual for a white Bostonian. The young Charles absorbed this nondiscriminatory behavior, and he took it to heart, particularly after entering the Boston Latin School. There his wealthier classmates ostracized him because of his humble background, and he learned early the personal sting of class discrimination.

Sumner graduated from Harvard, traveled to Europe, and eventually settled into a lucrative law practice at No. 4 Court Street in Boston. But by the 1840s he had grown disillusioned with the trappings of professional success. He read *The Liberator*, and although he did not believe in Garrison's views on politics and the Constitution, he did believe in the abolitionist principles of freedom and equality for all Americans. He wanted to use the law and the political system to end slavery, which he viewed as morally wrong and counter to the Constitution.

Sumner also believed in the universality of peace and equality, and he was growing increasingly frustrated that more people did not share his views. At a Fourth of July celebration at Tremont Temple in 1848, he was roasted by his fellow attorneys when he gave a speech on the virtues of morality in politics. To Sumner, like many abolitionists, the slave system was not only taking over American politics and economics, it was also taking over the hearts and minds of the American people. When a new political party, the Free Soil Party, came into being in 1848, Sumner was among its original and most faithful supporters. Slavery should not be permitted in the new Western territories, Free

Soilers argued; the new American frontier should be based on free enterprise, not slave labor. To Sumner, America's future depended on its moral adherence to the principles of freedom and equality set forth in the Constitution.

The same year he joined the Free Soil Party, Sumner had a chance to put his dedication to universal freedom to the test. In February 1848 he was approached by a twenty-four-year-old black attorney named Robert Morris. The Salem-born Morris had studied law in the office of Latimer's attorney, NEASS cofounder Ellis Loring. In 1847 Morris became the second black man in the country to pass the bar exam. As the only practicing black attorney in Boston, he knew firsthand how the evils of racial inequality did not merely enslave black people—it sought to keep them a permanent underclass as well. While traveling by coach with the Loring family from Salem to Boston, he'd been forced to sit on the roof of the carriage, since racial custom prevented blacks from sitting next to whites on public transportation. When he went to argue his first case, his opposing counsel, a white attorney, shook his fist in Morris's face and swore to "give him the devil." It was then, as he cried alone in his office, that Morris vowed, "I would prove myself as a gentleman, and succeed in the practice of the law, or I would die."

Charles Sumner, one of the most skilled attorneys in Boston during the nineteenth century. Before he became a senator, he argued for school desegregation before the Massachusetts Supreme Judicial Court in 1849. The case, Roberts v. Massachusetts, was a landmark in civil rights, setting the stage for the school desegregation battle waged by abolitionists and black Bostonians during the 1850s. (Courtesy of the Boston Public Library)

Robert Morris, the second African American to pass the bar exam in the United States and the only practicing black lawyer in Boston during the 1840s. In 1849 he represented Benjamin Roberts, whose daughter had been denied entry to the white public schools. The case was eventually argued before the Massachusetts Supreme Court by Charles Sumner. Morris also helped William Nell organize a boycott of the all-black Abiel Smith School on Beacon Hill. (Courtesy of the Social Law Library, Boston)

Like Sumner, Morris saw the law as a means to achieve racial justice. He also saw a link between the abolition of segregated public schools in Boston and the abolition of slavery in the rest of the country. Since 1845, before he passed the bar exam, Morris had been working with local black abolitionists William Nell and John Hilton in the School Abolishing Party. Hilton was a veteran of community organization—he'd been a member of David Walker's Massachusetts General Colored Association and the initial supporter of William Lloyd Garrison during the community's protest against the ACS in 1831. Nell was also a veteran of black protest—as the son of William G. Nell, a Walker associate and deacon at the Baptist Church, Nell had stood outside at the window of the African Meeting House in 1832 as Garrison, David Child, and others founded the New England Anti-Slavery Society. He had worked in Garrison's *Liberator* office, and in 1840 he had sent a petition throughout the North Slope that urged an end to racial segregation in public education.

The School Abolishing Party continued Nell's fight for integrated schools by trying to use the legal system to end racial segregation. The party turned to white abolitionist attorneys to present a bill to the state legislature. Morris suggested his mentor, Ellis Loring, who in turn contacted Wendell Phillips, his friend and fellow attorney. Like Loring, Phillips was a son of the Boston aristocracy—his father had been the city's mayor, and as a student at Harvard he was the only man in his class who was picked up by a private carriage every Saturday morning. His law degree gave him great success, but like Sumner he quickly became disillusioned with the limits of his practice. His wife had converted him to abolitionism, and the shocking attack on Garrison in 1835, along with the murder of Elijah Lovejoy in 1837, forced him into action. Like Garrison, Phillips saw the Constitution as a document that condoned slavery; rather than take an oath on it, he closed down his law office and joined the ranks of the NEASS. A gifted orator whose speeches were profound yet easily understood by the public, Wendell Phillips was one of the most famous abolitionist speakers in the country.

On behalf of the School Abolishing Party, Phillips and Loring presented a bill to the legislature that would make it illegal to exclude any child from a public school. As the bill went before the Joint Standing Committee on Education, Nell, Morris, and Hilton led the School Abolishing Party's community-wide boycott of the all-black Abiel Smith School on Beacon Hill. Unfortunately, the two-pronged assault was not enough—the bill passed, but it was not the law that the abolitionists had proposed. It did not make segregated schools illegal; instead

An engraving published in the abolitionist newspaper **The Anti-Slavery Standard,** *showing a black family being turned away from a white school. During the 1830s and 1840s, as William Nell, Robert Morris, and Charles Sumner waged their battle against segregated public schools, this kind of scene was typical. (Courtesy of the Boston Athenaeum)*

William Nell, the leading black advocate of school desegregation in Boston. As a child, he attended the Smith School when it was still located in the basement of the African Meeting House. At the age of twelve, denied the prestigious Franklin Medal for scholastic achievement because of his race, he vowed to "hasten the day when the color of one's skin would be no barrier to equal school rights." Despite the segregated education he received at the Smith School, Nell went on to become a respected historian; he was the first black historian to publish a book in 1855, entitled **Colored Patriots of the American Revolution.** *(Courtesy of the* **Massachusetts Historical Society)**

of allowing children to sue if they were excluded from a public school, it allowed a child to sue for money if he or she was denied a public school education. Since black children had a public school—albeit a poorly funded and educationally inferior one—this law would do little to help black parents who wanted to sue the school committee for equal access to white public schools. Disappointed but not stymied, the abolitionists went back to the drawing board.

Robert Morris, like William Nell, Wendell Phillips, and all the abolitionists involved in the integration of the public schools, was determined to use the law to fight for racial equality. He finally got his chance in 1848, in a case that would join him with Charles Sumner and push the abolitionist movement toward a new challenge to the racial status quo.

MORRIS'S CLIENT WAS BENJAMIN ROBERTS, a black printer. Roberts's four-year-old daughter, Sarah, had been denied entry to five white public schools in the city and was forced to attend the all-black Abiel Smith School on the North Slope of Beacon Hill. Roberts wanted to file a lawsuit against the Boston School Committee, using the new law, so that Sarah could attend the white school closest to her home. Morris took the case, and he asked Charles Sumner for help.

Morris and Sumner quickly realized that they were not merely arguing for the rights of Sarah Roberts—they were taking on a segregated Boston institution, the public school, which had a long history of denying equality to black children. If they won, the victory would integrate the city's public schools—but it would also take the abolition movement to a new level by ensuring that, once free, blacks and whites would enjoy equal access to public education.

This was no small task, since the state of black education in Boston was dismal in 1848. Still, the drive by black parents to get their children a quality education was fierce. For them, illiteracy was a sign of enslavement. The first thing free black Bostonians had done after the state abolished slavery in 1783 was to petition the state legislature for money for their own school. (Although slavery had ended, racial discrimination was rampant, particularly in the public schools, where black children faced horrendous abuse and discrimination at the hands of white teachers and students.) Although the school committee refused to give money for a black school, it did give black Bostonians permission to start their own school, though not until 1798. Until 1806, when the school moved to the basement of the new African Meeting House, classes were held in private homes, in carpenter shops, and in storefronts, with black volunteer teachers.

The biggest problem in those early days, of course, was money. The African School, as it was called, was a private school with a steep fee, twenty-five cents per month, which many North Slope residents could not afford. Thus, while the white school committee put money into the first state-run public school system for white children, black sailors raised two hundred dollars to keep the African School running as black parents, clergymen, and community leaders donated their time and energy to acquiring desks, school supplies, and books. It wasn't until 1812 that the school committee finally agreed to make an annual contribution to the African School, but it was far smaller than the amount allotted to white schools.

A brief light in the lives of black schoolchildren appeared in 1815 when one of their teachers, Prince Saunders, convinced a wealthy white

The Abiel Smith School opened in 1835 and was the first schoolhouse in the country built specifically for the purpose of educating black children. Before 1835, black students were educated in the African School, which was held in the basement of the African Meeting House. Although black citizens were happy that their children could attend a public school, its inferior curriculum and resources, insufficient funding, and segregated status led black parents to boycott the school and demand equal education for their children. After the city's public schools were desegregated in 1855, the Smith School closed. (Courtesy of the Boston Athenaeum)

merchant, Abiel Smith, to give five thousand dollars from his estate to the African School every year, both while he lived and after he died. The school committee finally agreed to take over the administration of the school, now called the Abiel Smith School. Black Bostonians had a reason to rejoice—thanks to their efforts, Boston was one of the first northern cities in the country to run a public school for black children.

With Boston running separate schools for black and white students, however, a new set of problems quickly surfaced. Money remained the biggest issue—the Abiel Smith School received less than half the funding of the Phillips School, the all-white public school located just a few blocks away on Beacon Hill. There was also the matter of the curriculum. Black students at the Abiel Smith School learned basic reading, writing, and mathematics, but they did not have the same art or literature courses as white students. School supplies were scarce, and books were even scarcer. The inequities were apparent at grammar school graduation. No black child from the Abiel Smith school went on for high school at the prestigious Latin School, unlike the white children who attended the Phillips School just two blocks away.

There was also the issue of who would be responsible for teaching black students. At the private African School, black teachers had taught black students, and although the conditions were hard, the leadership experience that black teachers gained by teaching at an all-black school was life-altering. John Russworm, the first black college graduate in the country, had taught at the African School; Russworm often credited his teaching experience with giving him the skills he needed to found the first black newspaper in the country, *Freedom's Journal*, in 1827. Also, since black teachers were not allowed to teach at white public schools in the city, the African School had provided jobs to well-deserving, highly educated black men and women who would otherwise have been forced to take jobs much below their intellectual capabilities. The African School had nurtured the small yet influential educated class of black Bostonians in a way that no other institution in the city would.

Yet the all-white school committee did not respond to either complaints about the inferior conditions at the Smith School or calls for the continued employment of black teachers, who were immediately fired without explanation and replaced with white teachers. The school committee's neglect of the Smith School was further compounded in the minds of black parents and community leaders when the white teacher, Rev. William Bascom, was seen coming out of a brothel during school hours. Bascom was also accused of acting inappropriately toward some of his female students, but complaints by black parents were not enough to sway the white school committee—it defended Bascom and accused the female students of low moral character.

In 1832, however, the school committee was forced to listen when a white man published a scathing report on the horrible treatment black children received from the public school system. David Child (the husband of Lydia Maria Child) helped found the New England Anti-Slavery Society that same year, and his report was full of abolitionist zeal. One of Child's criticisms was that the Abiel Smith School was still housed in the basement of the African Meeting House, where children were crowded into one room and forced to learn in conditions that were not tolerated in the white schools. Overcrowding, lack of books and supplies, overworked and underpaid teachers—Child outlined it all, including the fact that the local privy was located right next to the Smith School's play yard, which spread diseases and contributed to a bad odor in the classroom. Child recommended a bold solution—that the city should take some of the money it gave to the white public schools and redistribute it to the Smith School.

Tired of the constant complaints from black parents and pressured by the embarrassing findings in Child's report, the school committee finally did something: it built a new Abiel Smith School on the corner of Belknap Street and Smith Court in 1835. Almost from the beginning, however, it was clear that this school was not on a par with white schools. For one thing, the new building was overcrowded: proof was obvious to anyone who saw the scores of black children lined up on Belknap Street, waiting to enter the building every school day. It was the only public school in the city without a play yard, trees, or shrubs. And because it was the only black school in the city, black parents from all over Boston had to send their children to Beacon Hill if they wanted them to go to school. Children from far-flung parts of the city had to walk through the rain, snow, sleet, and cold; many, like little Sarah, passed numerous white schools on their journey. As the only public school offering black people an education, many adults, unable to read or write, relied on the Smith School to teach them as well. They arrived at night for lessons, overworking the teachers, whose pay was less than half that of their counterparts at white schools.

While white students learned composition, history, bookkeeping, algebra, geometry, natural history, and drawing, black students at the Smith School learned only the most rudimentary subjects. And the inferior curriculum was compounded by lack of space and neglect from the school board. Each floor of the Smith School had a single classroom, in which all subjects were taught at once. The constant noise was surely enough to try the patience of even the most seasoned educator.

Although trying to learn in an environment of chaos was difficult, many black children succeeded. Regardless of their success, however, their achievements—unlike those of white students—were never mentioned in the local newspapers. And no matter how well they performed on their final examinations, they never received the Franklin Medal, the award that the school committee handed out each year to high-achieving students. It had been the denial of the Franklin Medal that prompted twelve-year-old William Nell to promise that he would "hasten the day when the color of one's skin would be no barrier to equal school rights."

Clearly, Charles Sumner and Robert Morris faced a daunting task in 1848 as they set out to prosecute the school committee on behalf of

Sarah Roberts. When Sumner agreed to help Morris, two generations of disappointment lay behind them. They took the case all the way to the Massachusetts Supreme Judicial Court, where Sumner's argument became a landmark in the annals of American civil rights. He pointed out that there was no legal precedent for segregated schools in Massachusetts, since the state constitution guaranteed equality to all men, regardless of race. He also stated that racial segregation was un-Christian, especially in a country like America where all men were born equal. "Since, according to our institutions, all classes meet, without distinction of color, in the performance of civil duties," he concluded, "so should they all meet, without distinction of color, in the school, beginning there those relations of equality which our constitution and laws promise to all."

The argument did not sway the court, however. In his ruling, Justice Lemuel Shaw set the precedent for federally sanctioned racial segregation that would haunt the country for more than sixty years. As long as facilities for the races were equal, he stated, they could indeed be separate. In his view, the state had no right to dictate the intermixture of blacks and whites.

What seemed like a blow to the abolitionists at the time was actually one step in a larger, and ultimately successful, battle for racial integration. In 1843, five years before Sumner argued before the state Supreme Court in the Sarah Roberts case, abolitionists submitted two bills to the legislature that would integrate railroads and legalize interracial marriage.

Riding to and from abolitionist rallies across the North, black and white men who spent years speaking together on platforms could not sit together in railroad cars. In protest, they organized the first sit-ins in American history, riding together in the black section despite protests by the train's conductors. Garrison published a "Traveler's Directory" in *The Liberator*, in which black riders told of their experiences on the railroads, rating companies according to their treatment of black passengers. Some railroad companies were shamed into changing their policy by the constant airing of their discriminatory practice. Those that weren't faced a boycott by the city's abolitionists.

As the battle over the railroads continued, a battle over interracial marriage began. A state law prohibiting the marriage of blacks and whites was the only law in the colonial slave code to survive after slavery ended in 1783. In 1836 the legislature went one step farther and made any interracial marriage null and void, even if the couple had been married elsewhere. To abolitionists, the ban on interracial marriage and the segregation of railroads were glaring injustices caused by racial inequality. Abolitionist allies in the legislature linked the two issues by voting on the two bills at the same time—one bill to legalize interracial marriage, the other to desegregate railroad travel across the state.

In 1843 a legislative committee heard arguments by abolitionists for the desegregation of the railroads and for the repeal of the state's laws against interracial marriage. In the first case, Ellis Gray Loring once again led the charge. He argued that since railroads were funded, protected, and regulated by the state, the legislature had the right to intervene. And since the state of Massachusetts forbade "distinction in public privileges among different classes of citizens," it could rule that railroad segregation was unconstitutional. Testifying with Loring were Robert Morris and Charles Lenox Remond. Remond was a world-renowned black abolitionist who had traveled to Europe in 1840 to attend the World Anti-Slavery Conference. He told how he traveled all across England on the railroads without being separated from white passengers—unlike in his own country, where he had lived and paid taxes for his entire life but was treated like a second-class citizen. Hearing Remond's story, many legislators were moved to act. The legislature ruled that all segregation on railroad cars within the state of Massachusetts were against the law.

In the case of interracial marriage, popular opinion, as in the George Latimer case, won the day. Since 1839, thousands of people had petitioned the legislature urging repeal of the anti-intermarriage law. Thus in one year, the Massachusetts legislature forbade racial segregation in all intra-state transportation and allowed black and white men and women to marry. These two rulings were of monumental importance, given that the nationwide abolition of slavery was still more than twenty years away.

With these two successful blows against segregation, abolitionists were determined not to give up on the public schools. A boycott of the Abiel Smith School was organized in 1850 during which black men and women formed alternative home schools for their children. The election of some abolitionist supporters to the school committee during the 1850s also softened institutional support for integration. The question of school segregation was finally being talked about in abolitionist circles, in the black community, and on the school committee. The boycott continued, and in 1853 abolitionists again filed suit on behalf of a black child who was denied entry to the white public schools. In this case, the child was a light-complexioned boy named Edward Pindell, whose skin color allowed him to "pass" in a white public school. When school officials discovered that he was black and expelled him, his father filed a lawsuit. The school committee formed a subcommittee to investigate. With the school boycott still raging, and abolitionists still protesting, the school committee finally caved in.

Finally, in 1855, Boston became the last town in Massachusetts to formally desegregate its public schools. It was a victorious moment for Boston abolitionists, a moment that assured them of the triumph of equality over racial subjugation. But the high of victory would not last long, for Boston, like the rest of the country, was about to enter its most turbulent decade since the American Revolution.

CHAPTER THREE

The Turbulent 1850s

FROM THE OUTSIDE, THE HOUSE AT 66 Southac Street did not look like an arsenal. Certainly it was a busy place, with people of all colors coming and going during the day and sometimes into the night. It was a boardinghouse whose proprietors, Lewis and Harriet Hayden, were the most well-known conductors on the city's Underground Railroad. Still, by looking at the building one could hardly guess that it housed a small cache of weapons.

Southac Street itself was a busy place. Just up the street from the Hayden house stood the Twelfth Baptist Church, the largest black congregation on Beacon Hill; like the African Meeting House two blocks away, it was a safe haven for abolitionists to plan, argue, and organize. Leonard Grimes, the church's pastor, lived on the corner, where he cemented his congregation's reputation as the Fugitive Slave Church by counseling the city's small population of escaped slaves. On the corner of May Street stood the gaming house of John Coburn, a black businessman who provided financial support for the abolition movement. And down toward West Cedar Street stood the offices of John Rock, a black doctor and dentist who administered medical help to fugitive slaves. The fugitive slave church, the constant flow of financial and ideological support to the abolitionist cause, the cache of weapons in the house on Southac Street—all of these measures were taken by the black residents of Beacon Hill to form mass resistance against the Fugitive

Slave Law, which had recently been enacted as part of the Compromise of 1850.

The Compromise was aimed at appeasing both the antislavery North and the slaveholding South, but the result was a set of laws and ordinances that angered everyone and pleased no one. In response to the issue of whether new states should be admitted to the Union as slave or free, Congress pleased the abolitionists in the North by admitting California as a free state. Utah and New Mexico, however, would be admitted as territories in which slavery would be decided by popular vote. For slaveholding Southerners, Congress also passed a law prohibiting the federal government from interfering in slave trading between the states, a measure that ensured that even though the international slave trade had ended decades ago, the interstate trade would allow slave traders to keep earning their living.

When Northerners complained that such a measure was immoral, Congress quickly added two more provisions. Slave traders could trade, but not in the District of Columbia. Also, slavery in the capital itself would end, but only with the consent of Maryland residents.

The last part of the Compromise was the most devastating for black people, free and slave, and for abolitionists across the North. It created a Fugitive Slave Law, which made it easier for slaveowners to recover "property" that escaped to the North. Under this law, the burden of proof was on the fugitive, not the slave catcher, to prove his or her freedom, and because it was a federal law, all prosecution of fugitive slaves would take place in federal court under federal judges. If the judge ruled in favor of the slave, he was paid five dollars by the government; if he ruled in favor of the slaveowner, he received ten dollars. All personal liberty laws, like the one passed in Massachusetts as a result of the George Latimer case, were null and void. And assisting a fugitive slave was a federal offense, punishable by a fine and up to six months in federal prison.

For black Bostonians, like more than half a million free black people across the North, the Fugitive Slave Law was a death knell for the nominal freedom they had enjoyed for more than fifty years. The very real fear was that loved ones would be kidnapped from the street— since few people had free papers, especially in Massachusetts where slavery had ended over sixty years before, any black person was suspect, fugitive and free alike. Of the nearly two thousand black people in

Boston, few had ever been slaves, and those that were fugitives had enjoyed freedom for years. They went to church, they worked hard, they tried to raise their children well, but now their quest for total freedom was more elusive than ever.

One response was escape. The Twelfth Baptist Church lost half its members when more than two hundred people, many of whom had lived in Boston for decades, picked up everything and moved to Canada. Most black people, however, did not have the money or the resources to start over in another country. Many were also adamant that they should stay in their homes and fight. On October 4, they met at the African Meeting House and formed a group called the League of Freedom. Together, its members vowed to protest against the capture of fugitives and to protect themselves at all costs.

The logical choice for president of the league was Lewis Hayden, who assumed the post with the courage and valor that had characterized his life since his arrival in Boston four years earlier. Born a slave in Lexington, Kentucky, Hayden had experienced firsthand the horrors of slavery. After his mother was driven insane by the sexual harassment of a white slaveowner, his owner traded the young Hayden for a pair of horses. As an adult, he watched helplessly as his wife and two young daughters were sold, an incident that continued to haunt him despite his personal achievement. He remarked, "I have one child who is buried in Kentucky, and that grave is pleasant to think of. I've got another that is sold nobody knows where, and that I never can bear to think of." The mastermind of his family's sale was none other than Kentucky senator Henry Clay, who had founded the American Colonization Society over thirty years before and who had been one of the architects of the hated Fugitive Slave Law. No doubt the knowledge of this fact made Lewis Hayden's battles for the rights of fugitive slaves an emotional and personal one.

In 1844 Hayden and his new wife and child had managed to escape from Kentucky with the help of a white Ohioan named Calvin Fairbanks and Vermont abolitionist Delia Webster. After a harrowing journey that took the young family from Ohio to Canada, Lewis and Harriet Hayden found freedom in Detroit, where Lewis helped organize the Colored Methodist Society. Lured by the abolition movement to New England, he moved to New Bedford and then, in 1846, to

Lewis Hayden, one of the leading "conductors" of the Underground Railroad in Boston. His house on Southac Street (now Phillips Street) on Beacon Hill was a gathering place for fugitive slaves and their allies. Hayden is most famous for his involvement in the harrowing rescues of William and Ellen Craft, Thomas Sims, Shadrach Minkins, and Anthony Burns. In 1859 he was appointed messenger to the secretary of state, the highest position appointed to a black man at that time in history. (Courtesy of the Boston Athenaeum)

Boston. There he worked as a clothing dealer on Cambridge Street while his wife turned their house at 66 Southac Street into a boardinghouse for fellow black migrants. It was the Hayden house that kept a cache of weapons beneath its front steps, which Lewis threatened to ignite should a slave catcher demand entry into the home.

As a leader in the community, Lewis Hayden was both a man of the people and an intelligent ally of the white abolitionist community. As such, he served as a valuable liaison between the black masses and middle-class white abolitionists such as Wendell Phillips. When a group of white abolitionists met at the African Meeting House on October 14 to form the Boston Vigilance Committee, Hayden convinced members of the League of Freedom to join. Together, blacks and whites would raise money to help fugitives and to fight the Fugitive Slave Law in court. The Vigilance Committee had more than two hundred members from the white abolitionist community—men with money and resources to challenge slave catchers in the courts and in the streets. Members included Francis Jackson, Austin Bearse, and

Unitarian minister Theodore Parker. Lewis Hayden and John Rock were the only black members.

The Boston Vigilance Committee—with Lewis Hayden acting as a conduit between the black and white communities—was one of the most visible organizations of the Underground Railroad. As a highly organized system of blacks and whites who conveyed fugitive slaves from bondage in the South to freedom in the North and West, the Underground Railroad had been the stuff of legend since the eighteenth century. Free blacks, poor whites, and even other slaves had long helped black fugitives make their way to freedom—since the seventeenth century—but it wasn't until the end of the American Revolution that organized assistance for runaway slaves began. Such organized assistance was so common that in 1786 George Washington, himself a slaveowner, noted that a society of Quakers had been formed in Philadelphia to help a fugitive slave from Virginia.

With the advent of the steam railroads in the 1830s, abolitionists and slaveholders finally had the means to describe the secret system of transporting fugitive men and women to freedom. Many slaveholders were dumbfounded that black people, whom many proslavery advocates deemed content with their lot, defiantly ran off and stayed gone, despite every effort to find them. In 1831 a Kentucky slaveowner remarked that his slave, Tice Davis, must have "gone off on an underground road" after he fled across the Ohio River and disappeared into thin air. From then on, until slavery was abolished in 1865, the intricate, highly involved covert network became the most powerful means by which abolitionists and enslaved blacks defied Southern slavery.

In Boston the Underground Railroad was strong, but it was not the stuff of folklore and urban legend. Covert underground tunnels, secret passageways, hidden cul-de-sacs—these certainly existed, but more important to fugitives was the well-organized system at work above ground, in churches, living rooms, and back parlors of the North Slope. Fugitives arrived from Philadelphia, New York, and New Jersey to seek further distance between themselves and the South, and what they needed from Boston abolitionists was food, clothing, jobs, and sometimes train fare to cross the Canadian border. They also needed lawyers, such as Charles Sumner, Ellis Loring, and Robert Morris, to defend their rights in court. And they especially needed safe places to stay, such

William (right) and Ellen Craft, pursued in Boston under the federal Fugitive Slave Law of 1850. They escaped from slavery in Georgia in disguise, the light-skinned Ellen as a white man and William as her black slave. When slave catchers arrived in Boston to arrest them, William barricaded himself in his clothing store and Ellen was hidden by abolitionists on Beacon Hill. They were eventually transported safely to England, where they remained until after the Civil War. (Courtesy of the Boston Athenaeum)

as Lewis Hayden's boardinghouse, and churches, such as the Twelfth Baptist and the African Meeting House, through which they could form new roots within the community. Thus, by 1850 the Underground Railroad as a network of abolitionist freedom fighters and militant activists had existed for decades; and it got only stronger with abolitionist resistance to the Fugitive Slave Law.

Just eleven days after the Vigilance Committee had its first meeting, a slave catcher from Macon, Georgia, secured a warrant to arrest a fugitive slave couple under the new law. The names of the fugitive couple were William and Ellen Craft, and their story had charmed abolitionist audiences across New England and instilled pride in blacks across the city. On a rice plantation in Macon, William worked for a cabinetmaker, while Ellen worked as a ladies' attendant. Their lives were relatively easy compared to those of their fellow slaves who did backbreaking labor in the rice fields, yet the indignity of being owned by another human being was enough to prompt the Crafts to escape. As William explained, "It is true our condition as slaves was not by any means the worst. But the thought that we couldn't call the bones and sinews that God gave us our own, haunted us for years."

On December 21, 1848, after two years of marriage, the couple made their daring escape. Ellen, who was very fair-skinned, disguised herself as an infirm white man, while William pretended to be her faithful slave. They had obtained passes from their respective masters to travel to a nearby town for the Christmas holiday, and they used the money William had saved from his cabinet-making apprenticeship to pay for train tickets. Over the next four days they traveled as master and slave through South Carolina, North Carolina, Virginia, Delaware, and Maryland before arriving free in Philadelphia on Christmas Day. After staying briefly with a Quaker family in Pennsylvania, the Crafts arrived in Boston in 1849.

The network of black and white abolitionists in the city made the Crafts' assimilation into life on the North Slope appear effortless. With the help of Lewis Hayden and Leonard Grimes, William opened a cabinet-making business on Cambridge Street. Ellen's skills as a seamstress caught the attention of white abolitionist Susan Hillard, who agreed to teach Ellen upholstering in her home on Pinckney Street.

Ellen Craft, in the disguise she wore to escape from slavery in Georgia. After the Civil War, she and William returned to Georgia to start a school for newly freed slaves. (Courtesy of the Massachusetts Historical Society)

While saving money for an apartment of their own, the Crafts stayed in Hayden's boardinghouse on Southac Street. They were still there when a warrant was issued for their arrest on October 20.

Word of the impending arrest of the Crafts spread throughout the abolitionist community as quickly as word of George Latimer's capture had spread in 1842. But the Personal Liberty Law inspired by Latimer's case was of no use now, and a mob of angry white and black abolitionists met at the African Meeting House to form a plan. The most urgent need was to find another house for the Crafts to stay in: Hayden's boardinghouse was well known as a safe haven for fugitives, so slave catchers would logically look there first for their prey. At first Susan Hillard volunteered to take Ellen in, but George Hillard, her husband, also happened to be a U.S. Commissioner and hiding a fugitive would force him to resign. Immediately Vigilance Committee member William Bowditch hired a carriage and transported Ellen to Ellis Loring's house in Brookline; from there she was eventually taken to the home of Unitarian minister, and Vigilance Committee member, Theodore Parker. With Ellen safe, the Vigilance Committee began making arrangements to transport the Crafts out of Massachusetts.

Meanwhile, the North Slope of Beacon Hill had become a veritable armed fortress. William Craft barricaded himself in his cabinet shop on Cambridge Street with his fellow employees and a cache of guns and explosives so large that it scared off a slave catcher who came to the door. Houses up and down the hill were armed with swords, bayonets, and ammunition, while Lewis Hayden's house was filled with armed black men, prepared to light explosives should the U.S. Marshal force his way in.

While the North Slope went on the defensive, members of the Vigilance Committee began their assault on the slave catchers in their midst. They posted three hundred handbills across the city that described what the slave catchers looked like. To frustrate the slave catchers' activity, members of the Vigilance Committee followed them around town and harassed them, while the committee's lawyers filed complaints against them in court. By November 1, the bewildered Southerners had had enough. When Theodore Parker warned them that they would not be safe in Boston, they gave up and returned to Georgia.

But the abolitionists could not proclaim victory just yet. The warrant for the Crafts' arrest was still active; the couple would not be safe until they left the country. To prepare for their deportation, abolitionists Samuel May and George Thompson arranged for the Crafts to be sent to Liverpool, England, via Maine and Nova Scotia.

The rescue of William and Ellen Craft proved that the organized network of abolitionists across Boston and its environs was a force powerful enough to repel federal authorities. Yet it was not a victory they could afford to savor for too long: less than two months later, another fugitive slave once again found himself at the mercy of the new law. Unlike the Crafts, Shadrach Minkins had made the journey from Virginia to Boston alone, alternately hiding in the hull of a ship and walking in the frigid winter cold. He got a job at the Cornhill Coffeehouse downtown, a short walking distance from Garrison's *Liberator* office. He was working there in February 1851, when two Virginia slave catchers arrested him and took him to the federal courthouse.

Almost immediately, lawyers from the Vigilance Committee arrived at the courthouse to plead Minkins's case. They argued that he should be released since no proper cause had been given for holding him in custody, but their pleas went unheeded. Judge Lemuel Shaw, whose decision in the Sarah Roberts case two years before had upheld school segregation, ruled that Minkins could be returned to slavery under the Fugitive Slave Law. Just as Shaw gave his ruling, however, the courtroom erupted as more than fifty blacks stormed the proceedings and grabbed Minkins, still clad in his waiter's uniform, before any of the shocked attorneys and court officers could respond.

Among the mob of rescuers were Lewis Hayden, Robert Morris, and barbershop owner John J. Smith. They managed to bring Minkins to the home of an abolitionist, Rev. Joseph Lovejoy, in Cambridge. The Vigilance Committee arranged for Minkins's escape, and Smith and Hayden drove him by wagon to a safe house in Concord. The abolitionist community was as joyful as federal officials were furious. Abolitionist minister Theodore Parker praised the rescue as "the noblest deed done in Boston since the destruction of the tea," while President Millard Fillmore denounced the incident and demanded the arrest of all participants. Hayden and Morris were indicted, but they never served any jail time, and Shadrach Minkins arrived free in Canada, where he spent the remainder of his life.

Three black lives had been saved because of the dramatic and courageous work of Boston's interracial abolitionist movement. And the federal government was not about to let the citizens of Boston defy its laws. Slaveowners and their allies in the federal and state governments sought to prove that the Fugitive Slave Law was working by making an example of abolitionist Boston. Future fugitives would not be as lucky as the Crafts and Shadrach Minkins.

ON JUNE 2, 1854, THREE YEARS AFTER the rescue of Shadrach Minkins, a Boston fugitive named Anthony Burns was returned to his owner in Virginia after spending nine days in the city's federal prison. Within days of Burns's arrest, the Boston Vigilance Committee met to organize a plan of action, with abolitionists from all over Massachusetts attending a protest meeting at Faneuil Hall. They knew they had to act quickly. Just months after Minkins's rescue in 1851, fugitive Thomas Sims had been seized by federal marshals and returned to slavery, despite gallant efforts by abolitionists. Desperately, rescuers had placed a mattress below the jailhouse window so that Sims could jump to safety. But the plan had been foiled, and Sims returned to bondage. Now Anthony Burns was in the same courthouse, and proslavery officers were determined that he would meet a similar fate.

Burns had arrived in Boston from Richmond, Virginia, after spending three weeks stored amid the cargo of a shipping vessel. He worked at the Mattapan Iron Works in South Boston before getting a job at the clothing store of North Slope activist Coffin Pitts. Pitts had been a member of David Walker's Massachusetts General Colored Association, he was a deacon in the Twelfth Baptist Church, and in nearly two decades of unrelenting agitation for freedom, he had ministered to scores of fugitive slaves who stayed in his home on Belknap Street. On May 24, 1854, Anthony Burns had been walking home from Pitts's clothing store on Brattle Street when he was arrested.

Abolitionists realized that time was of the essence—the failure to rescue Thomas Sims had proved that, though legal maneuverings could delay the process, fugitive slaves would eventually be returned to the South. They had nine days to act, as federal commissioner Edward G. Loring—son of abolitionist attorney Ellis Loring—reviewed the case. If the abolitionists expected any leniency from the commissioner because of his family connections, they were sorely mistaken: Loring had Anthony Burns under heavy guard in the courthouse jail.

The Vigilance Committee held a meeting at Faneuil Hall two days after Burns's arrest. The Cradle of Liberty was filled to overflowing with black and white citizens eager to hear the committee's plan. All the best minds in the Boston abolition movement were there, including Samuel Gridley Howe, Leonard Grimes, Theodore Parker, and Robert Morris. All agreed with Wendell Phillips when he told the crowd that it was their duty to rescue Burns and any other fugitive that lived in the city. "Faneuil Hall is the purlieus of the court house tomorrow morning, where the children of Adams and Hancock may prove that they are not bastards," he cried. "Let us prove that we are worthy of liberty." The committee's goal was to organize a crowd to meet at the courthouse to rescue Burns from jail.

Prior to the meeting, another group of abolitionists met with Lewis Hayden and agreed to assign men to keep watch at the courthouse. They were afraid that the authorities, anticipating a repeat of the Minkins rescue, would try to transport Burns back to Virginia illegally before the judge gave his ruling. Hayden vowed that if Commissioner Loring ruled Burns must be returned to enslavement, as many people as possible "would crowd the streets when he was brought forth, and see to it that, in the melee which would inevitably follow, Burns would make good his escape." Back on the North Slope, Leonard Grimes and Coffin Pitts met at the Twelfth Baptist Church to organize a fundraising committee. Amazingly, they raised twelve hundred dollars, the price Burns's owner said that he would accept for Burns's release.

Suddenly, chaos erupted outside the courthouse. A mob of black men and women attempted to break down the doors. Immediately, the Vigilance Committee fled from Faneuil Hall to join the rescue attempt. Violence and mayhem ensued as angry abolitionists took a large timber and rammed it through the courthouse's west side. By the time order was restored, one federal officer had been killed and civil and military officials had been called in to control the crowd. The rescue attempt had failed, and the federal attorney voided Burns's sale to Grimes and Pitts, who desperately tried to pay the slave catcher the money they had raised.

On June 2, Commissioner Loring ruled that Burns should be returned to Richmond. The day marked one of the most dramatic moments in the city's history. Shackled and flanked by one thousand soldiers, Anthony Burns was led a third of a mile from the courthouse to a vessel waiting in Boston Harbor to send him back to Virginia. The spectacle passed by the Old State House, where Crispus Attucks had lost his life for the cause of American freedom more than seventy years before. It weaved past the Merchants' Exchange building into the heart of Boston's commercial district. Whether abolitionist, proslavery, or indifferent, most Bostonians were shocked. It had been more than sixty years since a slave had been publicly chained in Boston, and the sight brought home the ugly reality of the "peculiar institution." Over fifty thousand people crowded the streets, watching solemnly as Burns was led away. Some of them jeered and shouted at the officers escorting him to his doom. Samuel May, who had helped in the rescue of the Crafts four years before, ran a rope from the roof of his hardware store on the corner of State and Broad streets to the building across the street; from it, he and his sons hung two American flags turned upside down.

Undaunted, abolitionists immediately began to work toward the purchase of Burns's freedom. The Twelfth Baptist Church again took the lead, and within a year, Coffin Pitts, Leonard Grimes, and Lewis Hayden had raised enough money to buy Anthony Burns for thirteen hundred dollars. Finally, Burns's life was saved. Through the help of abolitionists, he enrolled at Oberlin College in Ohio; he then went to Ontario to pastor at a church for fugitive slaves. Yet the failure of the abolitionists to rescue him had brought home a terrifying fact: the more determined they became, the more bold and forceful their opposition became. The battle for the soul of America was no longer a matter for cool-headed organization and Yankee industriousness. It was a fight whose battles could be won only with blood.

CHAPTER FOUR

The War of Redemption

BLACK MEN, WOMEN, AND CHILDREN sat in the pews of the Twelfth Baptist Church on Southac Street. It was June 3, 1856, and they were solemn. Less than two weeks before, on May 22, Charles Sumner, one of the leading white allies of the fight for black freedom, had been brutally beaten on the floor of the Senate chamber in Washington, D.C. The reason for the assault was Sumner's "Crime Against Kansas" speech to the Senate on May 18. In it, Sumner had denounced the actions of proslavery expansionists, such as Illinois Senator Stephen Douglas and South Carolina Senator Andrew Butler, who wanted to extend slavery into the recently created Kansas territory. Sumner called such a move "the rape of a virgin territory." Kansas, he stated, was far more advanced than Senator Butler's South Carolina, "for throughout this infant Territory there is more mature scholarship far, in proportion to its inhabitants, than in all [of] South Carolina." Sumner concluded that Kansas, as a free state, "will be a 'ministering angel' to the Republic when South Carolina, in the cloak of darkness which she hugs, 'lies howling.'"

The speech would go down in history as one of the most eloquent denunciations of slavery in the history of the Senate, but to most Southerners Sumner's words attacked their principles and their honor. South Carolina Representative Preston Brooks, enraged at the assault on his state and his uncle Butler, found Sumner writing in the Senate

Chamber and beat him mercilessly with his cane. The attack stunned abolitionists across the North. As Sumner recuperated in seclusion, black citizens of the North Slope met at the Twelfth Baptist Church to express their indignation and to commend Sumner's long service to black Boston.

Sumner's "Crime Against Kansas" speech, and the incident it provoked, was rooted in the controversy that arose over the Kansas-Nebraska Act of 1854. The bill was designed by Senator Stephen Douglas to permit slavery in Kansas territory by a vote of popular sovereignty. Almost overnight, the prairie of eastern Kansas became a battleground for pro- and antislavery forces as Free Soilers struggled to claim the land as a free state. By 1856, armed resistance between the two sides reached a fevered pitch, as antislavery settlers at Lawrence, Kansas, were attacked by proslavery settlers from nearby Missouri. Three days after the assaults, a bearded militant abolitionist named John Brown led a group of antislavery guerillas in a deadly attack on Southern settlers on the Pottawatomie River. Bleeding Kansas, as the attack came to be called, enraged proslavery forces across the country, while abolitionists applauded the gallant efforts of Brown and his followers.

In Boston, the events in Kansas had a profound effect on abolitionists of both races. For Charles Sumner, Bleeding Kansas emboldened him in a way that his loss in the Sarah Roberts case had failed to do. Elected to the U.S. Senate in 1851, Sumner was one of the leading advocates of American freedom in Washington, and the incidents in Kansas bolstered his belief that slavery could never survive in the western territories and that freedom was inevitable as the country moved closer toward civil unrest. As he recovered from the beating, his "Crime Against Kansas" became a battle cry for Free Soilers and other political abolitionists, and Sumner became one of the most famous abolitionist senators in the country. In Boston, Sumner was viewed as a hero, and his assault was seen as the first blows of what now seemed like an inevitable battle between the states. Meanwhile, in South Carolina, Preston Brooks received hundreds of canes from enthusiastic supporters, many of whom congratulated him for his defense of Southern honor.

With tensions over Charles Sumner's beating still raging, the federal government's attack on black liberty continued. In 1857 the Supreme Court ruled in the case of St. Louis slave Dred Scott. The ruling was yet another victory for the South—it denied Congress's power to prohibit slavery in any federal territory, and it declared that blacks were not U.S. citizens. Abolitionists across the country were outraged. Black communities from Boston to Cleveland protested the ruling in churches and newspapers. In *The Liberator*, William Lloyd Garrison printed the headline "THE DECISION OF THE SUPREME COURT IS THE MORAL ASSASSINATION OF A RACE, AND CANNOT BE OBEYED." Garrison remained convinced that the struggle for black freedom was a struggle of "conscience against organized injustice." The Supreme Court's actions in the Dred Scott case seemed to support his idea that the Constitution supported slavery and that slaveholders controlled the government.

As had been true since the 1840s, many abolitionists supported Garrison's sentiments but they were also desperate for action. With Sumner bedridden, their chief ally in the federal government was gone. Speeches and protests were all well and good, but who was going to act? The answer came in the form of John "Ossawatomie" Brown, the grizzled abolitionist zealot of Bleeding Kansas.

Since his murderous retaliation against proslavery settlers in 1856, Brown had become a hero to abolitionists in New England. Although he had never belonged to any of the mainstream abolitionist groups in his wanderings across the North, Brown was a man with a vision. Like David Walker before him, Brown thought that freedom for black slaves was possible only through armed insurrection and that true redemption could be achieved only through an insurrection of blacks and whites against the evil forces of enslavement. Brown wanted to lead this insurrection, and in 1858 he began campaigning among Boston abolitionists for help.

His plan was to seize the federal arsenal at Harpers Ferry, Virginia, and form an interracial band of guerilla warriors to free the slaves in the surrounding area. Many abolitionists doubted that the plan would work, but they supported Brown's efforts. In Rochester, New York, Frederick Douglass warned Brown that his plan would fail, but he also introduced him to a black fugitive named Shields Green, who would eventually join Brown at Harpers Ferry. In Boston, many abolitionists came to Brown's assistance. Lewis Hayden later boasted that he gave Brown the names of black men who would be willing to follow him to Virginia, while Southac Street businessman John Coburn donated money to the fight.

The biggest supporters of the effort were six wealthy white abolitionists, later dubbed the "Secret Six," who had enough money and connections to give John Brown what he needed. Three of them—Franklin Sanborn, George L. Stearns, and Gerritt Smith—were from outside New England. The remaining three—Theodore Parker, Thomas Wentworth Higginson, and Samuel Gridley Howe—were Massachusetts men whose roots in the abolition movement were deep.

Theodore Parker was a Unitarian minister whose fame as an abolitionist preacher was legendary throughout Massachusetts. As a member of the Vigilance Committee, he had helped transport Ellen Craft to safety in 1850, and in 1854 he had helped Lewis Hayden and other abolitionist militants organize the guards who stood outside Anthony Burns's jail cell. Like many abolitionists, the Burns case made Parker more determined and more militant than ever. He believed that the days of peaceful discussion and moral reasoning were over. "I am a clergyman and a man of peace," he told his fellow abolitionists at Faneuil Hall in 1856. "But there is means and there is an end; Liberty is the end, and sometimes peace is not the means toward it."

Parker was friends with Thomas Wentworth Higginson, a Unitarian minister whose strong views on equality got him kicked out of his pulpit in Newburyport. He had helped storm the courthouse during the attempted rescue of Anthony Burns in 1856, and he had journeyed to Kansas to help the Free Soilers. It was there that he met Brown, whom he encouraged to come to Boston for help with his plan. Once Brown arrived, Higginson introduced him to Parker and to the final member of the Secret Six, Samuel Gridley Howe. Howe was president of Perkins School for the Blind, and his efforts on behalf of equal education for the disabled only increased his dedication to abolition. He ran for congress as a Conscience Whig and edited the antislavery newspaper *The Commonwealth*. His wife, Julia Ward Howe, the composer of "Battle Hymn of the Republic," was a seasoned abolitionist in her own right.

In March 1858, Parker hosted a meeting between Brown and the other members of the Secret Six. The men gave Brown money to finance his ambitious project and over the next year and a half wrote letters to keep him in contact with other abolitionist sympathizers. Finally, on October 16, 1859, Brown and his nineteen followers raided the arsenal at Harpers Ferry. When they were subsequently caught and executed by federal troops, members of the Secret Six went into hiding. Angry Southerners and federal officials were determined to hold all supporters of John Brown accountable. Even the most famous exslave in America, Frederick Douglass, was not exempt. Although never as intimately connected to Brown as the Secret Six, Douglass followed their lead and fled to Europe, where he stayed until it was safe for him to return to New York.

John Brown's assault at Harpers Ferry and his execution by the federal government made him a martyr among abolitionists of both races. To mark the day of his death, black Bostonians closed their businesses and held a day of fasting and prayer. At the Twelfth Baptist Church, Leonard Grimes led prayer services throughout the day. That night at Tremont Temple, William Lloyd Garrison and Lydia Maria Child organized an interracial memorial service. Despite his ambivalence about Brown's violent methods, Garrison delivered a stirring eulogy that forever cemented Brown's martyrdom in the minds of the country's abolitionists. "Today," he said, "Virginia has murdered John Brown; tonight, we here witness his resurrection."

EVEN AS JOHN BROWN'S EXECUTION marked a solemn end to the turbulent 1850s, a new day was dawning in Massachusetts. In 1860 John A. Andrew was elected governor by the largest popular vote of any candidate in the state's history. Andrew was a Maine man and Bowdoin College graduate whose law offices stood in the same building on Court Street where Charles Sumner had practiced before taking his seat in the Senate. Like Sumner, Andrew was a passionate abolitionist who strongly believed that the principles of freedom embodied in American institutions stood firmly on the side of emancipation for black people. As an attorney, he challenged the peculiar institution in any way that he could. For instance, in 1852 he helped a former slave arrange the purchase and release of his family from slavery in Virginia. As a lawyer for the Vigilance Committee, he helped defend the men indicted in the Anthony Burns rescue. And in 1859, as a relatively new state legislator, he helped prosecute slave catchers in Hyannis after a fugitive slave, Columbus Jones, was kidnapped and sold in Virginia. For

John Andrew, abolitionist, state representative, and governor of Massachusetts from 1860 until his death in 1867. As a lawyer, he worked for the Boston Vigilance Committee on the Anthony Burns case. He also helped fugitive slaves and their families purchase their freedom. As governor, he worked with black minister Leonard Grimes to start a home for elderly and infirm black Bostonians, which eventually became the Home for Aged Colored Women in Beacon Hill. (Courtesy of the Massachusetts Historical Society)

black Bostonians and their white abolitionist allies, the election of John Andrew signaled the end of the days when the state viewed the abolitionist philosophy apathetically.

Andrew's election could not have come at a better time. The election of Republican president Abraham Lincoln in 1860 signaled the end of negotiations between slaveholding states and the federal government. When Confederate forces attacked Fort Sumter in 1861, white citizens saw in the ensuing Civil War an epic battle over secession, economics, and states' rights. Yet in Massachusetts, black and white abolitionists saw the war as an epic battle between good and evil, redemption and damnation, freedom and enslavement. As Governor Andrew traveled the state, garnering support for the Union cause, he reiterated this theme to the people. "I have never believed it to be possible," he said, "that this controversy should end and peace resume her sway until that dreadful iniquity has been trodden beneath our feet." A deeply religious man who often gathered abolitionists in the State House to pray, he concluded, "I believe that God rules above, and that He will rule in the hearts of men, and that, either with our aid or against it, He has determined to let the people go."

Andrew's words were especially meaningful for black Bostonians and their free brethren across the North. "The contest must now be decided and decided forever," Frederick Douglass shouted from the pages of his Rochester newspaper. "Which of the two, Freedom or Slavery, shall give law to the Republic? Let the conflict come!" At Boston's Twelfth Baptist Church, just two days after Lincoln issued a call for Union Army volunteers, black citizens held a meeting and pledged fifty thousand black troops to the cause. They declared, "Our feelings urge us to say to our countrymen that we are ready to stand by and defend the government with our lives, our fortunes, and our sacred honor."

But the issue of black enlistment in the Union Army was just as controversial as the integration of the Boston public schools had been less than a decade before. The Civil War was seen as a "white man's war," in which blacks were not welcome. Many Americans believed that the war would last only a few months, and the idea that blacks could help quell a southern rebellion seemed ludicrous. When blacks in Washington, D.C., held a rally in support of the war effort, the Secretary of War curtly replied that their services were not needed.

In Boston the issue of black enlistment had been a topic of discussion since 1854, when William Nell led a petition by North Slope residents asking the legislature to integrate the state militia. When that effort failed, Nell and Robert Morris petitioned the legislature to create a black military company, which they called the Massasoit Guards. Not until 1859, shortly after John Brown's ill-fated raid at Harpers Ferry, did the legislature, led by John Andrew (then a state representative), propose a law that would prohibit the exclusion of blacks from the state militia. Governor Nathaniel Banks vetoed the measure, and once the Civil War started in 1861, the drive to admit blacks to the state militia took a backseat to the recruitment of white soldiers.. Most white Bostonians agreed with Lincoln's assertion that the war was about the preservation of the Union, not slavery. As such, black soldiers did not fit in with the Union's vision of the Southern conflict.

Undaunted, black Bostonians continued to assert their rights to bear arms for their country. Robert Morris organized a meeting at the Twelfth Baptist Church in which he urged the repeal of laws across the North that prevented blacks from joining the military. He and other black Bostonians saw the absurdity of excluding black men at the very moment that the country needed them the most. "If the Government would only take away the disability," Morris said, "there was not a man who would not leap for his knapsack and musket . . . and make it intolerable hot for old Virginia." Just weeks after the shots were fired at Fort Sumter, William Nell led a group of black men in organizing their own drill society on Boston Common.

Boston's white abolitionists agreed with John Andrew and Frederick Douglass that the war was chiefly about freedom for the millions of enslaved blacks in the South, yet they worried that Lincoln's focus on preservation of the Union would ultimately sacrifice the cause of black emancipation. They wanted Lincoln to acknowledge that the war was about abolition, with preservation of the Union a secondary goal. As Charles Sumner stated before a group of Republicans at the Boston Music Hall, "It is often said that war will make an end to slavery. This is probable. But it is surer still that slavery will make an end of the war."

In 1862 it became clear that Lincoln was starting to recognize slavery as a deciding factor in the war. In July he shared with his cabinet the preliminary draft of his Emancipation Proclamation, which stated that all "persons held as slaves" in states that were in rebellion against the Union as of January 1, 1863, would be free. It also said that the army and navy of the United States, which had previously been used to suppress slave rebellions, now would assist slaves in any efforts they made to secure their freedom. When Lincoln published the proclamation in September, Boston abolitionists were elated, but questions remained. Would the Emancipation Proclamation go far enough, since it did not free slaves in the Border States or say anything about the social and political equality of black people? Governor Andrew expressed the apprehensions of abolitionists across the city when he stated, "It is a poor document, but a mighty act." Both he and William Lloyd Garrison lamented the fact that the document delayed emancipation until January—and that it did not make slavery illegal.

Despite their misgivings, January 1, 1863, marked a momentous occasion in the city of Boston. Church bells rang to mark the enactment of the Emancipation Proclamation, while black men, women, and children crowded into the churches of the North Slope to hear sermons and speeches from their leaders. A gala at the Boston Music Hall was attended by blacks and whites from across the state. William Lloyd

Garrison, Robert Morris, Lewis Hayden, Wendell Phillips, William Nell—all were in the crowd, which cheered for the freedom that seemed closer than ever before.

The Emancipation Proclamation did not explicitly say that blacks could enter the Union Army, but it did say that all freed slaves could enter the army as laborers. This created a brand-new opportunity for black enlistment, which black Bostonians were quick to recognize. In November 1862, just weeks before the Emancipation Proclamation took effect, Lewis Hayden invited Governor Andrew to his house for Thanksgiving dinner. The two men had been friends since the Boston Vigilance Committee was created in 1850, and Andrew had used his connections to appoint Hayden messenger to the Secretary of State, the highest appointment ever held by a black man in the country's history. In the house at Southac Street that Thanksgiving of 1862, Hayden urged the governor to use the new Militia Act to create an all-black regiment in Massachusetts. Andrew agreed, and just days after the Emancipation Proclamation gala, he went to Washington to get permission from Secretary of War Edwin Stanton to raise a regiment of black volunteers.

Over a decade before, the call by William Nell, Robert Morris, Benjamin Roberts, and Charles Sumner for the integration of the Boston public schools had united black and white abolitionists in a battle against racial segregation and inequality across the city. Now the call for the creation of the 54th Massachusetts Regiment united black and white abolitionists in the effort to make emancipation the central focus of the Civil War. Governor Andrew began by asking for help from his good friend George L. Stearns. Stearns had been one of the Secret Six who had financed John Brown's raid in 1859, and now he took charge of a committee to oversee the recruitment of black troops across the North. He worked with Lewis Hayden to raise money for publicity, and within weeks abolitionists of both races had raised more than five thousand dollars for nationwide recruitment. The effort involved some of the most famous names in black abolition, including Frederick Douglass, Charles Lenox Remond, and Robert Morris. William Nell traveled as far west as Indiana to urge black men to come to Massachusetts to enlist. Beacon Hill barber John J. Smith, who famously drove the carriage that carried Shadrach Minkins to freedom in 1851, eventually became head recruiting officer for all four of the black regiments that came out of Massachusetts during the Civil War.

Meanwhile, John Andrew met with Francis G. Shaw, his good friend and fellow abolitionist, to discuss the appointment of white officers in the regiment. Andrew was looking for men of good background who were not afraid to lead a group of black soldiers. He wanted men from the abolitionist community who had grown with *The Liberator* and the Massachusetts Anti-Slavery Society. Andrew eventually selected Francis Shaw's twenty-five-year-old son, Robert Gould Shaw, a Harvard graduate and captain of the all-white 2nd Massachusetts Infantry. After some hesitation, Shaw agreed to take the position.

While Governor Andrew and Robert Gould Shaw discussed the logistics of training and equipment for the 54th Regiment, Wendell Phillips and Frederick Douglass held a meeting at the African Meeting House to rally black support for the regiment. This was no small task, since black enthusiasm for the 54th was at an all-time low. Two years before, when black Bostonians had offered their lives for the Union, whites in power had spurned their offer, telling them it was a white man's war. Now that the government suddenly changed its mind, many black Bostonians proudly refused to accept the offer. They were especially insulted that only whites would be allowed to lead the regiment. In a heated debate on the floor of the African Meeting House, Robert Morris spoke for many blacks when he objected to the continued use of the word white in the state and national militia laws. If black men were going to die for their country, shouldn't they be treated with equality? When Wendell Phillips tried to assure "Brother Morris" that black soldiers would be treated with respect, Morris snapped, "Don't call me brother until you have taken the word *white* out of the Constitution!"

Another matter that upset potential volunteers was recent news from the South. In December 1862, Jefferson Davis declared that all blacks found carrying arms would be handed over to state authorities and dealt with accordingly. This was a frightening prospect for black Bostonians, who knew that even if they were treated fairly by their white officers, their white enemies would not be as kind. They knew angry Southern white men saw black enlistment as a threat not only to their cause but to their principles, and they shuddered to think what might happen to them if they were captured. If Preston Brooks could beat Charles Sumner on the floor of the Senate simply for giving a speech, what might a Confederate soldier do to a black soldier who dared to hold a gun in defense of the Union?

Despite the indignation of some and the fear of many, black Bostonians began to warm to the idea of joining the 54th Regiment. Broadsides appeared on the streets, and rousing speeches were delivered from churches' pulpits, to encourage their enlistment. These efforts helped soothe black misgivings. By March 1863, black recruitment was up and support for the Union Army was at a fever pitch. More than 137 black Bostonians of military age (approximately 40 percent of the city's eligible black male population) enlisted in the 54th Regiment. Scores of men from Ohio, New York, Rhode Island, and Pennsylvania swelled their ranks, filling the one thousand uniforms of the regiment so quickly that John Andrew created a second regiment, the 55th, to accommodate all the volunteers.

The pride that the black soldiers of the 54th Regiment inspired in citizens of both races electrified the city as strongly as the rescue of Shadrach Minkins in 1851. William Lloyd Garrison and Wendell Phillips visited the regiment at its training camp in Readville, while black women of the North Slope's Colored Ladies Relief Society sewed flags and blankets for the men. Frederick Douglass's sons enlisted in the 54th, and Lewis Hayden's son enlisted in the Union Navy.

On May 18, 1863, the 54th Regiment marched through the streets of Boston, pausing at the State House, where Governor Andrew, Frederick Douglass, William Lloyd Garrison, and thousands of cheering citizens saluted their victory. A young black sculptress, Edmonia Lewis, took a cast of Colonel Shaw's head before he and his men marched to Battery Wharf to board their ship for South Carolina. On July 18, Colonel Shaw and hundreds of his black soldiers were killed at the battle of Fort Wagner, where the gallantry of the black soldiers in the face of bloody defeat became a source of pride for Bostonians of all races. The battle also produced a hero by the name of William H. Carney, a black sergeant from New Bedford, Massachusetts. After being shot several times, Carney bravely rescued the Union flag from desecration by stuffing it into his shirt as he crawled through the bodies of his dead comrades to the safety of the Union lines. "The old girl never touched the ground, boys," Carney said to his fellow soldiers as he presented the battered flag. Robert Gould Shaw would be buried in a mass grave with his soldiers on James Island; Carney would become the first black recipient of the Congressional Medal of Honor in 1900.

The work of Boston's abolitionists did not end with the deployment of the 54th Regiment, however. When the War Department refused to pay black soldiers the same as white soldiers, John Andrew and other abolitionists devised a way to use money from the state militia to pay the Massachusetts men their salaries. The black soldiers of the 54th refused, deciding on principle to go without pay until the War Department paid black and white soldiers equally. For eighteen months, they served without pay, prompting Boston's abolitionists to hold fundraisers and food drives for the black families left destitute by the noble act of their husbands, fathers, uncles, brothers, and sons. In June 1864, Congress finally agreed to equalize pay for black and white soldiers.

In addition to assisting the war effort, Boston's abolitionist community rallied to support the thousands of newly emancipated slaves in the South. The invasion of Port Royal, South Carolina, by Union troops in 1862 caused white landowners to flee, leaving thousands of black free people on the fertile, rice-growing coast. White abolitionists in Boston viewed this as a chance to prove to the rest of the country that black free people could work more profitably than when they were enslaved. Immediately, Boston abolitionists created the Boston Education Commission to help the newly free people of Port Royal make the transition from slave labor to free labor. Governor Andrew served as president of the commission, which collaborated with the abolitionist American Missionary Association in New York. Over the next fifteen years, organizations such as the AMA and the Boston Education Commission would transport thousands of black and white abolitionists to the South to help educate and uplift the former slaves.

Abolitionists also continued to support the poor and destitute in Boston. In 1860 John Andrew, Thomas Wentworth Higginson, and others founded the Home for Aged Colored Women directly across the street from Lewis Hayden's home on Southac Street. The plight of elderly black women had long been a concern of Leonard Grimes and Lewis Hayden. Homes for the elderly were strictly segregated in Boston. The Home for Aged Colored Women filled the need for quality care for elderly black women. Well into the twentieth century, it remained a symbol of the cooperation between black community leaders and white reformers.

The creation of the Home for Aged Colored Women, the foundation of the 54th Regiment, the continued support by black and white abolitionists for the Union effort—Boston's abolitionist spirit was thriving in the 1860s, and by the end of the Civil War it was clear that its principles were finally spreading to Washington. In 1865 the Thirteenth Amendment to the Constitution was ratified, legally abolishing slavery. After more than two hundred years of slavery on North American soil, the government was freeing more than four million black people. In Boston, celebrations across the city marked the occasion. On Cornhill, the offices of *The Liberator* were closed. Black Bostonians rejoiced, and white abolitionists applauded themselves for a job well done. They believed that the valiant battle for American liberty, which started with the fire of David Walker's *Appeal* in 1829, had finally come to a triumphant end.

CHAPTER FIVE

New Frontier, New Problems

IN 1865, AS POLITICIANS IN WASHINGTON struggled to draft the fourteenth amendment, which would grant citizenship rights to black Americans, Massachusetts became one of the first states to enact a Civil Rights Law that prohibited segregation and discrimination in public facilities. Although far from perfect, the law signaled for many Bostonians the beginning of a new era. When the federal government formed the Freedmen's Bureau at the end of the war to provide relief and education to freed people and their children, Boston already had a ten-year history of educating black and white children together in its classrooms. As race riots exploded across the South, black Bostonians proudly boasted that Lewis Hayden held a job in the State House, that black veterans held positions at the highest level of the federal Post Office, and that black men were graduating in record numbers from law school at Harvard and Boston universities.

With the Civil War over and slavery abolished, the country braced itself for new challenges. How could a country so thoroughly divided-begin to put itself back together? What would become of the millions of newly free men and women, and the hundreds of thousands of black people in the North who had been discriminated against for centuries? The country was unprepared to answer these questions, as Reconstruction took hold, ended, and the subsequent battle for racial equality propelled the country into the twentieth century.

Yet, even as William Lloyd Garrison ended his reign as editor of *The Liberator*, and abolitionists across Boston patted themselves on the back for a job well done, the radical spirit that began with David Walker's *Appeal* in 1829 continued to change the country. The battle for racial equality would continue into the twentieth century. Wendell Phillips, Frederick Douglass, and other carried the abolitionist spirit from the streets of Beacon Hill to the halls of Congress and the hearts and minds of a new generation. Charles Sumner's battles in the Senate for a national Civil Rights Law and the Fourteenth Amendment, guaranteeing civil equality to all Americans, forced a new generation of American politicians to live up to the true meaning of the country's creed. Women veterans of the abolitionist movement, including Lucy Stone and Elizabeth Cady Stanton, would use the methods they had learned fighting racial inequality in Boston to fight gender inequality across the country. And thousands of civil servants and educators, weaned on *The Liberator* and the antislavery societies, journeyed South to start schools, churches, and hospitals for the freed people.

The light that was lit in the schoolroom of a black church on Beacon Hill was slowly spreading across the nation. The country would still remain fractured and true racial and social equality would take another century to achieve, but as long as the abolitionist principles of America's past kept burning, the ability of the country to repair itself would never be lost.

SOURCES

"An Article on the Latimer Case." From *The Masssachusetts Law Reporter,* March, 1843. Boston: Bradbury, Soden, and Company, 1843.

"Argument of Charles Sumner, Esq., Against the Constitutionality of Separate Schools in the Case of Sarah Roberts v. the City of Boston Before the Supreme Court of Massachusetts." Boston: B. F. Roberts, 1849.

Atlantic Monthly, The. Various issues, 1880–1882.

Brown, Lois, ed. *Memoir of James Jackson: The Attentive and Obedient Scholar, Who Died in Boston, October 31, 1833, Aged Six Years and Eleven Months, By His Teacher, Miss Susan Paul.* Cambridge, Mass.: Harvard University Press, 2000.

Clifford, Deborah P. *Crusader for Freedom: A Life of Lydia Maria Child.* Boston: Beacon Press, 1992.

Colfax, Richard. *Evidence Against the Views of the Abolitionists, Consisting of Physical and Moral Proofs of the Natural Inferiority of the Negroes.* New York: James T. M. Bleakley, Publishers, 1833.

Collison, Gary. *Shadrach Minkins: From Fugitive Slave to Citizen.* Cambridge, Mass.: Harvard University Press, 1997.

Cromwell, Adelaide. *The Other Brahmins: Boston's Black Upper Class.* Fayetteville: University of Arkansas Press, 1994.

Daniels, John. *In Freedom's Birthplace: A Study of the Boston Negro.* Boston: Houghton Mifflin, 1914.

Dorman, Franklin A. *Twenty Families of Color in Massachusetts, 1742–1998.* Boston: New England Historic Genealogical Society, 1998.

Grover, Kathryn, and Janine V. da Silva. "Historic Resource Study: Boston African-American National Historic Site." Boston: National Park Service, 1999.

Hart, Albert Bushnell, ed. *Commonwealth History of Massachusetts.* New York: Russell & Russell, 1966.

Hinks, Peter P. *To Awaken My Afflicted Brethren: David Walker and the Problem of Antebellum Slave Resistance.* University Park: Pennsylvania State University Press, 1996.

Horton, James O., and Lois E. Horton. *Black Bostonians: Family Life and Community Struggle in the Antebellum North.* New York: Holmes and Meier, 1999.

Horton, James O., and Lois E. Horton. *In Hope of Liberty: Culture, Community and Protest among Northern Free Blacks, 1700–1860.* New York: Oxford University Press, 1997.

Jacobs, Donald M., ed. *Courage and Conscience: Black and White Abolitionists in Boston.* Bloomington: Indiana University Press, 1993.

Kendrick, Stephen, and Paul Kendrick. *Sarah's Long Walk: The Free Blacks of Boston and How Their Struggle for Equality Changed America.* Boston: Beacon Press, 2005.

Levesque, George A. *Black Boston: African-American Life and Culture in Urban America, 1750–1860.* New York: Garland, 1994.

Liberator, The. Various issues, 1831–1865.

May, Samuel. *The Fugitive Slave Law and Its Victims.* New York: American Anti-Slavery Society, 1861.

Mayer, Henry. *All on Fire: William Lloyd Garrison and the Abolition of Slavery.* New York: St. Martin's Press, 1998.

Pleck, Elizabeth. *Black Migration and Poverty: Boston, 1865–1900.* New York: Academic Press, 1979.

Richardson, Marilyn. *Maria W. Stewart, America's First Black Woman Political Writer.* Indianapolis: Indiana University Press, 1987.

Still, William. *The Underground Railroad.* 1870; reprint, Chicago: Johnson, 1970.

"Stories of the Fugitive Slaves." *The New England Magazine* 8, no. 5, July 1890.

Strangis, Joel. *Lewis Hayden and the War Against Slavery.* New Haven, Conn.: Shoestring Press, 1999.

Sumner, Charles. "The Crime Against Kansas," in *The Works of Charles Sumner.* Boston: Lee and Shepard, 1870.

"Third Annual Report of the Boston Female Anti-Slavery Society." Boston: Isaac Knapp, 1836.

Von Frank, Albert J. *The Trials of Anthony Burns: Freedom and Slavery in Emerson's Boston.* Cambridge, Mass.: Harvard University Press, 1998.

Williams, George W. *History of the Twelfth Baptist Church, Boston, Mass., from 1840–1874, with a Statement and Appeal in Behalf of the Church.* Boston: James H. Earle, 1874.

INDEX